Poppy

LET IT GO

HOW TO STOP YOUR PAST
RUINING YOUR FUTURE

All the best

Joh Ken

About *Let It Go*

"I was absolutely blown away by the content of this book. So helpful and so insightful into the power of the mind."
~ Sian Chare (UK), Nurse

"After some traumatic events in my life, I became depressed, defensive and very angry at the world. David's programme changed my life forever. Once I learned to 'Let It Go' and embraced a more positive mind, I started living the life meant for me. Six years on, I still use the techniques David taught me to continue to live my best life. I am beyond grateful to David."
~ Beverley Davies (UK), Magistrate

"I have read a lot of self-development books over the years and this has to be the most engaging. From the moment I picked it up, I felt myself instantly becoming more focused and motivated. The way David explains how to overcome fears and limitations made me really optimistic about what I can achieve by letting go. I highly recommend this book: it really has made a life-changing difference."
~ Maurizio Pozzi (UK), Owner of One Sixty Coffee Bar

"An inspiring and positive read in so many ways, with lots of tools and methods that you can use time and time again. This book is like having a personal life coach right there in your pocket. Highly recommended."
~ Jacqueline Leet (UK), Psychotherapist

"Growth is only possible when you take steps deep inside, and needs courage, strength, grit, trust and faith in the process. The *Let It Go* programme made me aware of the pain that had become a part of my identity. It gave me more energy and internal strength to create a new future without the burden of the past."
~ Tiina Latikka (Finland), Professional Coach and Development Manager

"David's book and in-person courses are simply incredible. The techniques really helped me to change and give me the frame of mind to finally go for the goals which have been in my mind for years, overcoming the eternal feeling of 'not being good enough'. Thank you for the support!"
~ Jon Berg (UK), Business Owner

"This book is my bible! So many tools and strategies right at your fingertips to help in navigating and unlearning a system of limiting beliefs. It offers a wealth of strategies that are simple to follow and to practice, through which we can eventually create a new and healthy lifestyle."
~ Wendy Blanchard (USA), MS, CHHC, CPS, Holistic Health and Wellness Coach

"Having suffered with severe anxiety for many years, I thought that I would never have the courage to travel abroad. With David's help and using the techniques and tools that he has taught me, I have achieved what I thought what was impossible. Thanks to David, I now know I can CHOOSE calm."
~ Diane Hopkins (UK)

"Because of the guidance in David's book, my life has changed after decades of pain. I now truly love and respect myself."
~ Mary Morgan (UK), NHS EPP Tutor (for Pain Management)

"I love this book! Great scenarios and easy to read. It certainly makes you think about where your life is going and how you can help yourself for a better future. It's made a big difference in my working and personal life."
~ Karen Frayne (UK), Dental Nurse

"It's so refreshing to read a self-help book with a unique message. Applying the knowledge and practising the exercises in this book will provide quick, long-lasting results."
~ Clare Roberts (UK), Health Psychologist

"This year of 2020 and COVID-19 has been a challenging one for most people. The *Let It Go* book is going to help so many people 'let go' of emotional baggage which is making them feel unhappy. Personally, I think this book is perfect for anyone who's looking for ways to be happier right now!"
~ James Page (UK), Engineer

"David's positive and clear concept will literally enable the reader to make powerful healing changes to their mental well-being."
~ Tracey Hill (UK), Sales Consultant

"*Let it Go* is an energetic motivational journey led by David Rahman. It encourages honest exploration of the self, guiding the reader towards making positive shifts and achieving enhanced ways of being."
~ Nikki Cass (UK), Art Psychotherapist

"*Let It Go* is a must-read for anyone holding on to something in their life. It is full of scenarios and fantastic exercises that you can always come back to at any stage. David explains the process in a very simple way that is easy to understand."
~ Agnieszka Kasprzyk (UK), Mindset Coach

"Such powerful and simple tools to transform your thought patterns and your life! The perfect book to challenge your own mind and take you from oppressed living to complete freedom!"
~ Elizabeth Hood (Australia), Principal & Director, Elite Real Estate

"What a happier world it would be if people read David's book and 'Let It Go'. Following the practical techniques and examples laid out in the book will lead to more positive, confident and healthy people, encouraging others to do the same."
~ Phil Clubley (UK), Kinesiologist

"I had lived with Clinical Depression for 34 years and M.E./ Chronic Fatigue for 20 years when David entered my life and taught me the tools to 'Let It Go'. From the first day of following David's programme of practical techniques, there was a noticeable improvement in both mind and health; after six weeks, I was no longer using a wheelchair! I still live with M.E./Chronic Fatigue but am now in control of the symptoms rather than having them control me. David's techniques have not only given me my life back, but also given me a greatly improved mindset to live my life by. This book offers every person, whatever their situation, the opportunity to live a happier, less stressful, more satisfying life – it will prove to be the greatest gift you have ever given yourself."
~ Janine Gibson (UK), Business Partner

"This book is a life changer. It's definitely a book I will refer to again and again."
~ Sarah King (UK), Archive Manager

"The book conveys the complex psychological concepts in a way that is simple and easy to understand. The value of this book lies in the practical exercises and examples. They will help you be clear about how to let go of the un-useful things in your life."
~ Roxana Pana (Romania), Psychotherapist

"This book is a thoughtful inspiration. The use of words to explain the subconscious mind and the relatable examples make *Let It Go* a witty and insightful read. I can't wait for the world to gain awareness at the same time as they 'Let It Go'."
~ Gemi Bertran-Lant (USA), CEO, Nourish the Brain Institute

"If you want to gain a deeper understanding of how you yourself 'tick' – through practical and often challenging exercises – to change your life for the better, then this really is the book for you."
~ Russell Lawson (UK), The Ideas Distillery

"David Rahman's book is an excellent read. It's clear and so easy to understand. The title, *Let It Go*, is such a simple sentence, but so powerful. Reading the book, you feel that it has been written specifically for you. It was almost as if I had David right next to me helping me with day-to-day life. Because of this book, I feel like I have a new-found confidence in life. David encourages gratitude and I'm very grateful for him."
~ Nick Watkins (UK), Construction Estimator

"This book has really helped me to express my feelings and 'Let It Go' in a positive way. It made me understand that I am not the only one who carries this mental backpack around most of the time. David's book *Let It Go* is a must-read. I've found my motivation again."
~ Akeem Griffiths (UK), TV personality and Big Brother runner-up 2018

"Despite a deeply ingrained level of scepticism towards the 'wellness industry', I enjoyed *Let It Go* hugely. It is a practical, insightful – but above all, timely! – conversation with someone who becomes your friend on the journey. It is a guidebook to ways of thinking, as a first step towards embedding mental habits promoting confidence and happiness."
~ Phil Ashill (UK), Mentor at Business Wales and PRIME Cymru

"A must-read for achieving your best life! A complete understanding of how your thinking affects your behaviour may be impossible to achieve for most people in their entire lifetime. Working with David on the practical exercises in this book, you will actually get a lot further, much quicker, on your journey to achieve self-awareness, happiness, fulfilment, a sense of belonging, self-worth and positive self-image. Unlike many self-help books, reading *Let It Go* will help you feel ready to face the rest of your life with confidence in yourself and be proud of your life, wherever you are."
~ Edward van der Kleijn (UK), International Partnerships Director

LET IT GO

HOW TO STOP YOUR PAST
RUINING YOUR FUTURE

D A V I D   R A H M A N

First impression: 2021

This book is intended as a supplement to rather than a
replacement for medical and professional mental health care.

Some names in the Case studies
have been changed to protect privacy.

Cover design: Y Lolfa
Illustrations: Tay Noronha

ISBN: 978 1 78461 830 8

Published and printed in Wales
on paper from well-maintained forests by
Y Lolfa Cyf., Talybont, Ceredigion SY24 5HE
website www.ylolfa.com
e-mail ylolfa@ylolfa.com
tel 01970 832 304
fax 832 782

Contents

Acknowledgements

To my family and close friends. You are my oxygen. I love you. YNWA.

As in anything worthwhile in life, I believe you need continual support and encouragement to get through the times when you feel like giving up. Without the following people on the long journey to create this book, it would not have been possible. Thank you for your love, support, energy and commitment; but most of all your undying belief in me as a teacher and coach. When I didn't believe in me, you did. Thank you from the bottom of my heart. I am so grateful.

Angelina Mansell, Phil Ashill, Clare Roberts, Emma Jones, Emma Williams, Tony Vee, Nicki Vee, Tiina Latikka, Ewan Mochrie, Fiona Morgan, Maurizio Pozzi, Kelly Turner, Sebnem Onal, Sam Wheel, Nathan Browning, Adam Sheridan, Zoe McDonald, Alan Doyle, Dylan Parry, Catherine Price, Jon Berg, Aga Kasprzyk, Ruth Levene, Elizabeth Bryant, Jodie Grove, Jon Bunyan, Denise Brannan, Paul Wakefield, Juliet Sidney, Andrew Harris, Beverley Davies, The Finn Sisters

I am sure the minute the book goes to press, I will realise that I have missed some names off that list! But you know who you are, and I want to thank you for always being there.

This book has been influenced by the work of Keith Harrell, Tony Robbins, Robin Sharma, Joe Dispenza, Maxwell Maltz, Sonja Lyubomirsky, Richard Carlson, Deepak Chopra and Tony and Nicki Vee. I'm honoured to stand on the shoulders of these wonderful teachers. The work has also been influenced by many areas of study, including life coaching, psychology, cognitive behavioural therapy, counselling and mindfulness.

Thank you to Tay Noronha for producing amazing illustrations for the book, to enhance the content of each chapter.

And last but not least, much love and appreciation to the team at Y Lolfa – Carolyn Hodges, Lefi Gruffudd, Garmon Gruffudd, Robat Gruffudd, Alan Thomas, Gwenllian Jones and all the printers – who have worked tirelessly to get the book published in a year which has seen the world go through so much change, disruption and uncertainty.

David Rahman
December 2020

Foreword

As someone who at 47 years old discovered the unnecessary pain and suffering of 'Holding On', it is a joy to see a fellow sufferer in David work on himself to the point where joy and happiness are now his standard experience. It's super exciting that he has put pen to paper and masterfully scribed this book to share what he's learned along the way.

David is so right when he wonders, as I do, why this critical information is left off the curriculum in our education system. It has the potential to assist the next generation to live a life free of the mental and emotional pains and restraints that not understanding it causes us throughout our lifetime.

I love it that David has created a model with practical exercises to match. It is all so simple to follow and demonstrates the power of simply 'Letting Go'.

I encourage you to dive into this book with an open mind and trust the gift you will be rewarded with by not only reading it but joining in. It will allow you to live on a path where you too experience an ever-growing life of happiness and joy.

~ Tony Vee, Chairman of Master Coach
and founder of The 10-10 Movement

Introduction

Hello,

Firstly, thank you for taking the time to read this book.

We all carry what I call a mental backpack around with us. From time to time we need to empty it and free ourselves for a fresh start. This book examines what happens when we unload our emotional burdens from the past, start thinking differently and stop trying to exert complete control over our future.

I have taught the tools and techniques in this book with clients in workshops and seminars since 2005. Then in 2017, I started delivering the *Let It Go* programme to assist people in freeing themselves from the negative thinking which was stopping them living a life of happiness.

As a result of my sessions with them, so many people have remarked to me that the process of letting go should be taught to us at school. As we grow up, facing the trials and tribulations of the world, we are forced to make choices at lightning speed. By 15–16 years old, we are instructed to choose what career we'd like to follow. We are expected to make our choices and plan our future. So much pressure on a youngster to make huge decisions so quickly, so young.

As we move through our childhood, we accrue habits. We start to think a certain way, behave a certain way and react a certain way. Every decision and choice is based on our narrative of the world around us. We often struggle to understand ourselves, and become confused as to where we fit in with everything. Events and situations conspire to leave us feeling emotions ranging from hope to hopelessness. We form fears, and start to create stories of how the world operates. Our opinions shape our reality. Our perception of reality shapes the way we feel. The way we feel influences the way we behave.

Over time our daily conversation with ourself – or 'inner dialogue', as it is commonly known – can encourage or impede our progress from within.

Whatever we believe to be the truth becomes our truth. We will then do almost anything to justify, protect and prove what we believe is the truth.

As I grew up, I would often feel lonely and lost, and never good enough. I had little self-confidence and very poor self-esteem. The world appeared to me to be dark, grey and challenging. I felt I could not talk about these thoughts or feelings as it would make me appear weak and vulnerable and would be emasculating. At the age of 26 I had dark thoughts. Questions such as 'What's the point of me?' would frequently trouble me. I knew I had to go to war with my mind if I was to come out of this, yet sadly, I didn't know how.

I would fake confidence just to get by and 'fit in'. My life was a mixture of happy moments, anxiety, lack of confidence and uncertainty regarding the future. It was a rollercoaster of emotions.

Today, I am both happy and grateful. Happy with who I am, and grateful that I live my life with purpose, fulfilment and joy. Please don't misunderstand me: life is not easy. It is a work in progress. I believe everyone is a work in progress. The moment you stop working on yourself is the moment I believe your life plateaus. From that point there is a chance that you may slip backwards.

This book delves into the mechanics of the human mind. It will offer you an understanding of why we think as we do, and what has brought about this way of thinking. This I demonstrate by unveiling to you a model of thinking called the Blueprint Process. This is enhanced by a section which describes the FIT Mind Model®. All of this illustrates why letting go is an incredibly powerful philosophy, helping you live a joyful and fulfilling life.

The book provides you with a tool kit which you can utilise to help you let go. Letting go covers a wide range of issues, including fear, emotional reactions, past events and negative thinking. It also involves letting go of that 'story' which currently underpins your view of your own worth. This story is influenced by the events of your life and your interpretations of these events.

Finally, I would like to emphasise that this is written as a practical handbook for you to refer back to at any time. Make notes, highlight particularly useful passages and share any learnings with family and friends. Carry it around in your bag or briefcase. We all need reminders during those times of need. I do sincerely hope it helps you move forward, enabling you to live the life you deserve.

Here's to your health and happiness always.

Love and gratitude,

David x

I

Why Let It Go?

'Things which matter most must never
be at the mercy of things which matter least.'
~ Johann Wolfgang von Goethe

Learning to 'Let It Go' is fundamental to changing your life. I believe it is the key to helping people release themselves from the negative thinking which is currently keeping them feeling unhappy. It is easier said than done and difficult to install as a habit, and is something you need to commit to on a moment-by-moment basis. It's particularly tricky when it comes to releasing yourself from behaviours and deep thought patterns that have become habitual.

Think of something that you couldn't do previously, but which now you can do quite easily. It could be learning to drive, speaking a foreign language or cooking a three-course meal for important dinner guests. Think of something that you achieved that you never thought was possible. For me it was public speaking. The thought of it would produce sensations of panic and nausea. Why? If you think about it, when you're in front of an audience, your fears may include being judged, not being liked, looking stupid, fluffing your lines and not being interesting. To become an accomplished speaker, I had to let go of the limitations that I had imposed upon myself. Now I can easily speak in front of 10 people or 1,000 people.

Letting go could involve letting go of a conversation that you had this morning in the office with a certain colleague, which has left you feeling disgruntled. You start to replay the negative baggage from this conversation at various points in the day with a variety of people. Every time you discuss how you feel about 'that' conversation, it strengthens the anger and annoyance within you. By the evening, you find yourself at boiling point. Throughout the day you have received opinions from a whole host of people, some of which will have reinforced your anger, and others you will have chosen to ignore as you are remaining adamant about your version of the conversation. By the time you ready to go to bed, unfortunately your mind is entirely consumed with the events of the day. As a result, you are unable to fall asleep.

Have you ever had an experience like this? It is quite common for people to hold onto events well past the 'sell-by date', and as a result of not letting go, that person suffers a gamut of emotions which could have been avoided.

Let it go

Moving on, let's look at a few examples of needs, worries and habits that it might serve you well to let go:

- the need to be liked
- the need to be right
- the need to have the last word
- the need to feel successful in comparison with others
- the need to meet aggression with aggression

- the need to have your say on something petty
- picking over the past in your mind. 'Should have said...', 'Could have been...', 'Might have been different if...'
- the urge to 'think forward' to your future and insure against potential pitfalls
- the need to avoid being poor
- the need to control others
- the habit of asking yourself the same question, although the question itself is a self-perpetuating, negative loop: 'Why do my relationships keep failing after six months...'
- the habit of focusing on the negative: 'I hate my job, I hate my job...' rather than thinking, 'I would love a new job.'

Do any of the above resonate with you personally? Do you know anyone who exhibits any of these beliefs and habits, and would benefit from letting go?

The lure of self-limiting belief

Even when you can see that these habits are unhelpful, it can be tough to release them. Your mind automatically jumps in, asking, 'What can I grab hold of now?'

Invariably, unhelpful thoughts like these, no matter how seductive or 'realistic' they might appear, are rooted in faulty negative beliefs about yourself. Feelings of inadequacy or low self-worth underpin them all. They do not serve your best interests.

Take a moment to imagine how your life might feel different if you were to release yourself from these needs by shedding them completely. Can you even imagine a life which includes no ruminating over the past or daydreaming about your anxieties regarding your future? I have a little phrase to explain it:

In order to become who you are,
you need to let go of who you have been.

If someone cuts you up on the road, or pushes into the bus queue ahead of you, can you imagine shrugging it off? Could you allow your partner the last word in an argument, or let your mother-in-law's attempt to provoke you wash over you without getting agitated?

The reason that 'letting it go' is such a difficult thing to achieve is that no matter how dysfunctional a habit, and no matter how clearly you perceive its dysfunction, it is still deeply ingrained and automated, like a reflex. When you decide to resist it, shutting down your standard response to a situation and choosing a more conscious, active and empowering way to think or behave, you're laying the groundwork to forming new habits. But it's tough going at first. Don't expect it to be easy.

To be capable of doing this, you need a measure of self-awareness. You also need to think about why the unhelpful thinking has endured for so long. What is it that these unhelpful thoughts and behaviours 'do' for you, in a psychological sense?

Keeping yourself stuck?

There are many examples of this. A feeling of inadequacy or self-doubt can keep us 'stuck' in a bad relationship or unhappy work scenario. Fear of rejection may prevent you from asking someone out. Fear of the unknown may be so overwhelming that even a miserable situation feels preferable to the pain and uncertainty of cutting off from it.

One of the biggest and most damaging needs that people feel is the need to control other people. This always backfires, and leads to all manner of unhappiness. In extreme instances, people may adopt a bullying attitude towards others, without even being conscious of it. They may dominate their partner, trying to manage or control their behaviour. Of course, the very idea that one person can 'control' another, or – more importantly – that this is ever a desirable thing, is deeply flawed. Nevertheless, so many of us cling to the idea.

Letting go has as much to do with surrendering our anxieties about the future as it does with releasing ourselves from the past. When we think about 'letting go', it seems to imply a linear cut-off between the past and the present, but the ties that hold us back may equally be attached to anxious projections forward, to an imagined future. This is discussed further later in the book. These projections are uniquely damaging as they compromise our ability to see exciting opportunities when they present themselves.

Trying to second-guess the future (born out of a fear of change) means we're closing ourselves off from the liberating wide-open sense that anything could happen – which it could. But we need to free ourselves up from any sense of what we think must happen, may happen or is going to happen to really live at full capacity.

Even the hardiest amongst us fear change. Fear of the unknown is in part natural self-preservation and cautiousness. But it often becomes unhelpfully inhibiting. People take years to rethink their career or stick around in a bad relationship for decades, and this is all down to fear of change. Many people go to great lengths to avoid change (sometimes unconsciously), but once you push past your fears and embrace them, life becomes more meaningful. This will be discussed more in the Fear chapter.

Scenario I

I heard a helpful analogy recently at a conference. Imagine your life is a beautiful hot air balloon. It's waiting to take off. However, no matter what you seem to do, you're still on the ground. Then, as you peer over the top of the basket you're standing in, you immediately notice sandbags hooked onto the sides. These represent your doubts, fears, anxieties, the negative past or your obsessions about things needing to be perfect. You notice that there are sandbags labelled 'overly self-conscious', 'inconsistent', 'lack of trust in the future', 'avoidance' and 'low self-esteem' weighing the basket and the balloon down.

When we have these sandbags impeding our lift-off, we start to experience frustration, annoyance and fear of never living our life the way we'd like to. It is only when we let go of these sandbags that life starts to change. I urge you to question what is holding you down, and to make a decision to let go of this in order to change your life forever. It could be the best thing you have ever done.

It's often the case that once you've decided to make a change and take action, the original fear seems misplaced. You may come out with comments such as 'It wasn't as bad as I thought it would be.' Even if there is some fallout, the positive energy you've generated by committing to making a change gives you a new sense of perspective on the original problem or situation. It frees you up mentally, physically and emotionally.

Scenario 2

Imagine you are at the front door of a big mansion. You walk in through the front door. The house is airy and light. You approach a staircase and walk up it. At the top of the stairs there's a corridor that turns to the right. You walk along this corridor and you can see a door in front of you at the end of the corridor. You walk towards it and open the door. The room is a large bedroom, beautifully decorated with a large mirror on the wall. You walk towards it and stand about 12 feet away from the glass. Imagine looking into the mirror at your reflection. You see a vision of yourself as an old person. You are 80 or 90. Life is drawing to an end. Your hair is grey and your posture is slightly hunched. You look into your eyes in the mirror. The eyes of your reflection look back at you with regret. What is it that your 80-year-old self is trying to say to you? Why are those eyes so full of regret?

You notice that there's a red button on the wall next to the mirror. Underneath it is a sign that says, 'Press here to return to youth'. You look back and see the regret again. Most people would give anything to press that button.

The one thing we all want to avoid when we are older is regret. So I want you to run that image in your mind to remind yourself that without changing your present, you can't change your future. What would your older self advise you to change today in order to look back in years to come and not have any regrets?

Now is the time to change so that when you are 80 years old, you don't look back with regret. Stop putting things off. Now is moment to turn away from "I'll do it later."

Examining the Past

A head that's stuck in the past won't help you move forward. That's one of the reasons why I think traditional talking therapies can sometimes serve to keep you frozen in time. Please don't misunderstand me. Talking is the vital first stage to moving forward. However, when you're excavating your past, picking over the carcasses of past hurts, mining your memories for clues about what went wrong, you're holding onto your history with both hands. To take an everyday analogy, it's like attempting to clear out your house, but failing because you get sidetracked rereading all those old cards, refiling the photos and the paperwork, rearranging the books in alphabetical order. You end up more immersed in your past than you had been before, looking backwards all the time. Eventually we have to let it go…

In order to release yourself from the trappings of what's happened before, you need to force yourself to turn your back on it, to release the baggage rather than cannibalising it. That way you avoid the temptations of comparison traps: measuring your present situation against your past failures, fearful of tripping on the same stumbling blocks again. Letting go facilitates the fearlessness you need in order to gather the momentum that will propel you to a bright future.

Once you push past your fears and embrace them, you regain your autonomy. You'll feel as if you're back in the driving seat. But it does require a leap of faith, and that's why people resist change so forcefully. Keeping themselves stuck in painful, dysfunctional relationships, bad jobs, unhappy situations. It's the 'better the devil you know' thinking that persuades us to cheat ourselves.

Here's a little story to demonstrate how flawed thinking can endure for generations, totally unchecked.

One day, a young mother and her little daughter are preparing a joint of ham for roasting. The mother cuts off the end of the joint, hacking through the bone to shorten it before putting it in the roasting tray.

'Why do you do that?' asks the daughter.

'I don't know – I've always done it that way. Gran always did it that way.'

'Why?'

'I'll ask her.'

So the mum calls her mother, and asks her why she cut the end of the joint off before roasting it.

'I always did it that way. My mother did it that way too.'

In turn, she calls her elderly mother and asks her why she cut the end off the joint of ham.

'Because otherwise it wouldn't have fitted in my roasting tin,' she says.

It's a false example, but you can see how these habits and behaviours persist. And how nonsensical they often are.

Over to you

I can only give you the tools to help you change. It's up to you to do the work and reap the benefits. A chef can give you a recipe, but you have to follow it properly to reproduce it. The 'Let It

Go' recipe for change does work, but you've got to commit to it and put in the effort. If you do, you'll be able to make some profound changes in your life, like so many other people I have had the honour to help on their path to a happier future. But I can't stress enough that the work is continuous. There's no quick fix.

When you're feeling happy and in a good place mentally, you're more open to new possibilities. On the flipside, an angry, anxious or depressed person won't have that same mental flexibility and openness. Rigid, ingrained and negative ways of thinking close you off inside, so it's really important to disrupt and dislodge them.

A positive 'bring it on' attitude to change and the ability to let go of negative baggage are themselves magnetic qualities that will help you to generate positive energy, sending out happy vibes that will draw positive reactions from other people and attract good things towards you.

As you embrace letting go, and start to see and feel the benefits, it may be something that you could recommend to family, friends and loved ones in times of need.

You have to take positive action if you want to see some changes. The first step is to resolve to really let go of the thoughts and emotional baggage that are holding you back.

As the expression goes, 'If you do what you've always done, you'll get what you've always got.'

Exercise

Take a pad of paper and a pen and spend an hour or so thinking and writing about your unhelpful beliefs, fears and habits which are not serving you. Have a good think and take your time.

Think about where these started and what the thinking that underpins all of this is based on. Does it come from deep-held family patterns, social lessons learnt in the psychological swamp of adolescence? How many of these ways of thinking are helpful in any way to you now?

Put as much as possible down on paper. You may be surprised at what you write down. Being honest and transparent with yourself can be a somewhat cathartic experience as you seek to let go of the thoughts, habits and ways of being which do not serve you.

This is by no means an easy exercise. However, it is definitely worth your time and effort.

TIP: When you do start the exercise, ensure that you are in a place where you are unlikely to be disturbed. Switch your tech off. It's crucial that you are not distracted. This allows your mind to be calm and focused.

How will your life change if you let go of what is holding you back?

2

Your Blueprint

'You must have control of the authorship of
your own destiny. The pen that writes your
life story must be held in your own hand.'
~ Irene C Kassorla

Your 'Blueprint' is the operating system that runs you. It's
the web of invisible, habituated thought processes that
governs your reactions to every situation. As a result, it is the
single biggest influence on the way you experience life and
the world around you. Your Blueprint underlies all of your
relationships, your view of people, your perception of what's
possible. In essence it is born of all the events and influences
that you have experienced in your life, and the meaning and
interpretation that you have attached to them.

The trouble is that for the vast majority of people, this
operating system is deeply flawed. To run with the computing
metaphor a little further, it's full of glitches, bugs and viruses.
When a computer is new, everything works perfectly, just as
when you're born, your Blueprint is clear. But what happens
when you've had your computer for a while? You may
accidentally download a virus. The computer only does what
you tell it to do. You don't purposely download viruses. But
the faulty software (Blueprint) will then cause the computer
to malfunction. It may stop talking to the printer. You might
then blame the printer, but it's not the printer's fault.

Likewise, the faulty thinking that's become part of your Blueprint comes with its own convincing disguises (personality traits, bad luck, hard-bitten wisdom, someone else's problem). Over time, these insidious thought processes have become amalgamated into your thinking and have corrupted your logic. You've grown to accept the skewed version of reality they offer you as 'just the way it is'.

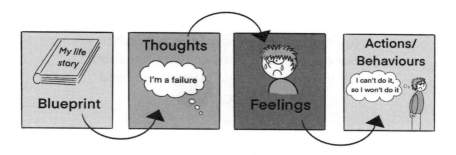

In the simplest terms, if you're thinking good thoughts, you will feel good. So when you wake up and think, 'It's a lovely day – the sun is shining!', your mood is positive. Your reactions to whatever happens to you will stem from that happy feeling. Similarly, if you're thinking, 'All men are bastards!' when you go on a date, no matter how much you're hoping it will go well at a conscious level, you're likely to be primed subconsciously for your date to slip up, or say something to confirm your worst suspicions. You have a checklist in your mind to tick off, reinforcing the thought that 'All men are bastards'.

 TIP: Take a photo of the Blueprint Process and store it on your phone. Discuss it with friends, and ask their opinion on its merit.

Scenario

Here's another example: imagine you've gone to a pub, and you accidentally knock over an angry man's drink. How is the angry man going to react? His Blueprint is primed for rage. There could be any number of reasons for this. He thinks angry thoughts and subsequently feels angry, and therefore when his drink is knocked over, he reacts angrily.

Now, we don't know why he's reacted angrily. Could it be that he's just found out that his wife has been cheating on him with his best friend? Or that he's been told he's got terminal cancer, and has only months to live? He's angry at life. We simply don't know why. We only see the tip of the iceberg of his emotional thinking. It is from this minimal information that we make a judgement about someone, as we almost never know what is going on under the surface of someone. What would happen if we let go of judging someone so quickly, and asked ourselves the question, 'I wonder what is going on under the surface of this person?'

Now I want you to consider your own pattern. Have you ever thought or heard yourself say the following?

- 'I have such bad luck with money/men/work.'
- 'The world is full of angry/lonely/impatient people.'
- 'I've never been any good at public speaking/ideas/being organised.'
- 'If there's flu going around, you can guarantee I'm going to catch it!'
- 'Just my luck. Nothing ever goes right for me.'

All of these thoughts are examples of problems in the Blueprint. The symptoms of this are the limiting and negative things you've decided about yourself, the world, and other people. You weren't born thinking this way. Instead, as a consequence of things you've experienced – many of them years ago in the distant past – you've unconsciously latched onto these negative perceptions and nurtured them, thereby ensuring they become self-fulfilling prophecies. They become your beliefs. Your **BS** ('belief system', that is!).

There's a phrase I like to use a lot: 'Where Focus Goes, Energy Flows'. It's one of the Power Statements that we'll be ready to introduce in a later chapter. It's fairly obvious when you think about it, but surprisingly easy to forget: the more you 'feed' something – whether it's positive or negative – the stronger it gets. Partly this comes down to confirmation bias (once you've decided on something, you see proof of it everywhere), but it's also a question of practice. You'll get better at the piano if you devote time every day to playing it. Conversely, you can also get very good at putting yourself down, and as a result decrease your self-esteem slowly over the years, draining your self-confidence. How you think is ultimately down to you.

Altering your Blueprint can lead to dramatic shifts in everything from self-esteem to relationship satisfaction and workplace success. Once you free yourself from your filter of negative and distorted thinking, new possibilities will offer themselves up to you.

The good news is that it isn't necessary to delve deep into your past and pick over the fossils of past hurts, striving to understand who did what and why and how you feel about it all. Of course, there is a place for this, but it requires a lot of time, money (all that therapy can be expensive) and patience (nothing is likely to get solved any time soon). For the rest of us, it's perfectly possible to facilitate deep transformations in thoughts and behaviour by committing to choosing healthier, more productive ways of thinking. View it as a project: practise your new habits every day, and you'll quickly start to see a difference.

If you're unconvinced, consider the following analogy:

You're driving along one day and your tyre runs over a sharp nail. You get a puncture and have to pull over. You have a number of choices about what to do next.

Do you stand there and examine the nail for the next three or four years?

Do you stare back down the road from where you came and wonder...

- If I'd left home at a different time, could I perhaps have avoided this?
- If I'd driven a different way, perhaps I wouldn't have driven over the nail?
- What if I'd stayed at home in the warmth of my comfortable living room?

Maybe you should be just fixing the tyre and moving on in your journey.

People are experts at looking back down the road from where they came and examining it repeatedly. What does this do? It simply means that they don't move on their life, as they're too busy looking at the past. It also creates an anxiety about moving forward in their future, for fear of 'driving over the nail' again.

Letting go is a far better use of energy, resources and time. Both approaches are likely to reduce your chance of repeating the same mistake again, but when you're consumed by the quest to unpick complex emotional wounds of the past, like an emotional archaeologist, you can easily get stuck. It's the ultimate distraction from the present, from the business of living – and if you aren't careful, it can leave you hanging in a state of suspended animation, indefinitely postponing moving on until you've tied up all those loose psychological ends. Which could take forever.

My aim, with this book, is to help you to draw up a new Blueprint for yourself that enables you to react in a way that serves you better. Simple.

The key point here is that the Blueprint underpins your thoughts. It triggers your thoughts themselves, and colours your perception of everything you witness. When you suffer from anxiety or depression, your Blueprint is conditioned to reinforce your dysfunctional view of the world by triggering more and more anxious or depressed thoughts. Of course, these feed back into the Blueprint, strengthening your conviction that the world is a worrying or depressing place. This is why it's so powerful.

Re→Act

It might be a little linguistically ugly to split this word in two, but it's a helpful way to unpick what's going on every time you think, feel, do or say something in response to a stimulus – whether that's a situation, another person or a piece of information. You're 're-{en}-acting' a stock response, based on your internal state and the behavioural habits you've honed over time (your Blueprint). You're bringing a whole lot of psychological baggage to each and every interaction you have and the first step to freeing yourself from the habit is to acknowledge it's happening.

Let's take an in-depth look at what your Blueprint is made up of:

- your values
- your personal beliefs
- your fears
- your memories
- your toxic-thinking-trap system

These are the 'files' that make up the software package (your Blueprint) which tells you how to think. This in turn controls the way you feel, and that defines the way you behave, act or react at any given moment. So if you are in a good mood, you are thinking positive thoughts and any action you take is based on this optimism.

So altering your Blueprint is multifaceted. It involves a readjustment to your values, beliefs, emotional needs, fears, your perception of your memories and your inbuilt blame system. It's deep and complex, but also simple, as it all comes down to one question: 'What do I really think, feel and need?' If you follow the exercises in this book, I'll walk you through the process and give you the tools you need to make it work.

All of that sounds analytical, but it's actually the opposite of that. So much of a faulty Blueprint is made up of skewed self-talk and bad logic – overthinking that has its own complex language and structure. The key to the process of letting go of all of this is to get back in touch with your deepest instincts and common sense.

The process outlined in this book is sequential and teaches wisdom through repetition. As you work through it, you'll learn new tools that will work together to help you rebuild a healthier, more functional Blueprint. Don't skip over any of it – work through the book in order and stick with it.

Approach this project with the unquestioning tenacity of a toddler learning to walk. She falls down, gets up again and keeps on going, time and again. She doesn't think, 'I'll do that next week...' or, 'I need to think about this a bit more before deciding on whether to try again...' There is no procrastination, no 'I'll do it later' to kill her aspiration.

This isn't to say that you won't stumble on the way. But failure is part of the process. So long as you keep on going, you'll get there. The biggest obstacles in your way are your fears – they come in many guises, like bespoke saboteurs, intent on disrupting your attempts to get on with life. They're like those annoying pop-ups you get when your computer has downloaded a virus, but many people have become so conditioned to them that they accept them as reality.

Fear has many faces and flavours. Fear of not being good enough. Fear of failure. Fear of the past. Fear of the future. Fear of dying. Fear of being ill. Fear of uncertainty. Fear of being found out. These fears pop up in an instant and are often triggered by the most off-the-cuff remark, insignificant request or suggestion. Remember, when you feel fear, it appears in the same place as when you have butterflies. Your tummy area. In physiological terms, there is a fine line between fear and excitement.

Behind all of these fears are memories. I think it's helpful to think of these as the clips and videos saved onto a Sky Box/ Tivo-style recorder in your mind. They're available to replay whenever you want. But the difference between your memories and the recordings on your Sky Box is that your memories all have feelings and emotions attached to them. Many of these emotions are negative, and fuel your fears and paranoias.

It's the nature of the Blueprint to try to weave all of these memories and associated emotions into a coherent narrative; to spot patterns and refer back and forward within the memory bank, drawing dissonant fragments of your life experience together to reinforce your Blueprint and confirm the very fears that limit you. There's a voice, constantly saying, 'See, I told you you were like this' or 'There you go, people always behave like that'.

In essence, your Blueprint is your perceived story of your own life.

Exercise

Let's call up a good memory to watch the process in action. Close your eyes and recall a great holiday you've had. Perhaps there was a perfect day on the beach that sticks in your mind, or a relaxed evening out with your partner or friends, where you drank cocktails and dreamed of future plans? Just thinking of those memories is likely to make you feel happier and a little bit lighter, even when you snap back to the present.

So it makes total sense that the more time you spend inhabiting negative memories, the more these will bring you down. I'm not concerned with the memories that you have. I can't change them, and neither can you, but you can stop reliving them all the time so that you don't automatically 'call up' fears and negative reminders.

Once you resolve to accept the past and move on, and start to apply the techniques in this book to your daily life, you will begin to see a powerful shift in the way that you experience things.

3

A Brief History of Beliefs

'You can have anything you want if you are
willing to give up the belief that you can't have it.'
~ Robert Anthony

Our Blueprint contains our beliefs about ourself and the world
around us. These core beliefs are our feelings of certainty.
They become ingrained within us. Three important beliefs we
possess about ourself are:

- Who we believe we are
- What we believe we are capable of
- Where we believe we fit in the world.

These beliefs influence our daily actions and behaviour. They
form the conversation which we constantly have with ourself.
A man may be desperately wanting to ask out a girl he has just
seen across the room. However, internally, his low self-belief
stops him in his tracks. As she leaves the bar with her friends,
he mentally kicks himself with annoyance.

Our beliefs shape our reality. So, where do they come from?
There are three distinct phases of the development of beliefs.

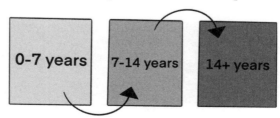

0–7 years old

From birth to 7 years old, beliefs are usually learnt from the people who are bringing you up. For most people, it is their parents. Whatever Mum and Dad tell you becomes your truth. You start to ask questions such as 'What colour is the sky?', 'Why do aeroplanes fly?' and 'What does that food on the dinner table taste like?'. Your curiosity causes you to ask question after question, and your belief system as a result expands. If your father follows a particular football team, you stand a high chance of supporting them too, and 'believing' them to be the best team in the land. You may be born in a certain part of the world where they have a belief that 'all homosexuals are going to hell'. This is something that becomes indoctrinated within you, and subsequently your behaviour adapts accordingly. You may be born in a country which believes that the cow is a sacred animal. Hence the thought of eating beef repulses you. What we are exposed to shapes our beliefs.

From 7–14

Where you do spend most of your time during this period? School. Therefore, who also starts to influence your beliefs at this time? Teachers and your peers. The time you spend in school forms the majority of your waking hours. As many of us have found out, the words that a teacher says to us can influence us for years to come.

Imagine Kyle, who is 8 years old. His teacher mentions to him in a throwaway remark that he is not as well behaved as his sister was when she was in the same class. Kyle is then told at the age of 12 that he is 'not as good at Maths' as his brother. He starts feeling and believing that he is not good enough. At 13 years old, Kyle becomes infatuated with a girl in his class. He asks her on a date a year later, but instead she goes on a date with his best friend. This further erodes Kyle's confidence. One day he joyously brings home a school report showing that he has achieved 87% in Mathematics. His mother questions what happen to the lost 13% of the marks. What was supposed to be a proud moment for him has turned into a scene of feelings of disappointment. Yet again he doesn't feel good enough. His confidence erodes further.

From 14 onwards

By the time Kyle has reached 18 years old, his confidence has diminished to the point where he has very little self-belief. This is compounded by fear of failure, fear of looking stupid and fear of being alone. Factors such as life events, social media, the media, TV programmes, movies, friendships and relationships have influenced Kyle over the years.

The example of Kyle shows what can happen to anyone. I share it with you to demonstrate how our belief system within our Blueprint develops over a relatively short space of time. In this case, Kyle has lost confidence and self-belief due to a series of disappointments over the years. Can Kyle go on to change his beliefs about himself? Yes, of course. It all starts with deciding to change. Two people may be brought up the same way and have the same experiences, yet develop into complete polar opposites. Our interpretations of what we experience in our formative years, who guides us and what action we take thereafter has a huge influence on this outcome.

Beliefs are there to be changed. From the dawn of time, beliefs about the world that we live in have kept changing. If you were born hundreds of years ago, you would be led to believe that the earth was flat. You were told that if you boarded a ship and travelled to the 'ends of the world', you would drop over the edge into oblivion. Faced with this belief at that time, would you board the ship? Most people would say no! Now we know the earth is round, we have no problems boarding a ship to sail across the ocean. How do we know the earth is round? The evidence we have includes satellite photographs, the fact that people have sailed and flown right around the world, and mathematical calculations involving the sun, moon and earth. These support our belief that the earth is round.

If you were to persist in telling people in the 1600s that one day men and women would fly, they would probably attempt to have you locked up. Today we have smartphones, bluetooth and WiFi. Imagine trying to explain these to someone just 25 years ago. You would be branded a fantasist and delusional. In this short space of time, what was recently thought of as science fiction has become science fact. A famous example is the bagless hoover created by the inventor James Dyson. Dyson was dismissed by all the well-known hoover manufacturers. After over 4,000 prototypes and 5 years, accruing over a million dollars in debt, Dyson went on to create a hugely successful and innovative company.

Often when we attempt to change a paradigm by shattering existing beliefs, we are met with resistance. This may be in the form of questioning and the pouring of cold water on the ideas we have of starting a business or running a marathon. Have you ever proposed anything and been met with scepticism? I remember when I wanted to start delivering workshops and speeches, the voice inside of me screamed words like 'No' and 'Why?' The night before I was due to give my first ever speech at a prestigious local hotel, I suffered a panic attack. I awoke drenched in sweat, with my heart pounding and body shaking. Now, years later, I don't experience those fears any longer. My belief about my fear of public speaking and being able to deliver a speech have disappeared. It did not disappear overnight. The work I had to put in to get rid of it took the form of repeatedly delivering speeches, seminars and workshops, even when I felt fear. We can disrupt and replace our beliefs when we take consistent action, and remain self-aware. I truly believe repetition births new skill and beliefs. It all, however, starts with taking action. In essence, we have to go to war with our belief system, systematically questioning it and taking purposeful action to move past any limiting beliefs and fears.

Scenario

Think of a time in your life when you were too afraid to do something. It may have been in your childhood. A rope swing was hung from a tree in the local park during the summer holidays. This new local attraction was very popular with the children in your street, as well as your siblings. Unfortunately, the thought of you swinging from this tree filled you with dread – you had convinced yourself that the rope would snap.

A year before you had watched an action movie in which there was a scene that had involved a rope snapping. Even though you had not dwelled on it, or so you thought, your subconscious mind had created a fear to 'protect' you from falling.

Over the summer you became frustrated and envious of the fun which the other children appeared to be having with the rope swing. They would holler and scream with delight as they swung from a high branch of the tree. They would also tease you as to why you were not joining in! Eventually, one Sunday evening, you'd decided to try the swing. There was no-one around, in case you made a hash of it!

As you nervously let go of the branch, clinging onto the rope, you felt a sense of fear and excitement at the same time. You also felt a sense of relief! After the rope had stopped swinging and had come to a stop, you gently lowered yourself down to the ground. You couldn't wait to try it again. The fear was gone. Your belief about the swing had changed.

The above is a true story. It happened to me back in the summer of 1978 when I was 10 years old.

Now I would like you to look back at any time in your life when you changed your belief about something, and by doing this you achieved a goal. Perhaps you didn't think you could find someone who could support and love you like you desired, but you did. Maybe you wanted to learn to drive, but never thought you would be able to pass your test. You did.

 TIP: Ask three trusted friends which of your beliefs they think perhaps don't serve you. For example, they may have noticed that you consistently mention that you are a 'victim of life'.

Over time, our beliefs are subject to change. Life events conspire to expose us to both success and disappointment. Our interpretation of these events influences this inner belief system. The great news is that you have the ability to take charge of what you believe. It all starts with the power of decision.

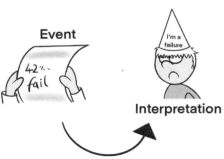

Exercise

List all the things that you would love to experience in your lifetime. This may include the places you'd like to see, people you'd like to meet, things you'd like to buy, projects you would like to accomplish and dreams you would like to achieve. For example, you might like to start your own business, enjoy a luxury five-star holiday, learn a new language or play an instrument.

List the reasons why you think you cannot achieve them. Write your answers down without editing or filtering your words. Just pour them out onto paper.

This will help highlight your invisible belief system which is stopping you from achieving your full potential. These things are what you need to work on letting go of.

4

What Is the Definition of Thinking?

'The minute we begin to think
we have all the answers, we forget the questions.'
~ Madeleine L'Engle

Most of the time, we take our thinking for granted. We let the mind get on with its own quiet business of making sense of the world around us, jumping to conclusions, skipping over some things and zoning in on others.

But have you ever been asked what the definition of thinking is? We say a multitude of things such as 'I'm an over-thinker', 'I was up all last night thinking – I couldn't sleep', or 'I'm going to think about where to go on holiday this year', but without using a dictionary, how would you try to define thinking? Basically, it is a series of questions and answers at lightning speed, combined with our interpretation of those answers, which then causes us to feel a certain way.

It is this constant Q and A session with ourself that leads to us feeling, behaving and acting in our own unique way. We can therefore conclude that the quality of your questions will determine the quality of your life.

What is the first thought that most people have on waking every morning? It's so obvious that the answer may escape you. The answer is that they normally wonder, 'What time is it?'

These days, people then reach for their mobile phone. At this point, after they have checked the time, many people will then go on to examine their messages, emails and social media. The distraction is so powerful that the initial enquiry about what time it is has then escalated into an avalanche of thoughts. These can potentially cause a variety of unhelpful negative emotions to rise up, depending on what's just been read. This is not what we ideally want first thing after waking up!

TIP: Keep an alarm clock by your bed and your phone well away from you first thing in the morning to avoid temptation.

The average person is said to have around 60,000 to 70,000 thoughts per day. However, a study by the National Science Foundation found that approximately 95% of our thoughts are unoriginal and repetitive. That means we are living our life like the movie *Groundhog Day*! Is there a certain truth in this? Imagine flying like a superhero over a city like London, invisible to the people below. As you fly over in the morning, you notice people travelling by train into the workplace. From overhead they look like ants. They generally go to the same office, have lunch at the same place, eat similar food every day, go home the same way from work, have dinner and a glass of wine, watch television and go to bed. Next day the process is repeated. Obviously there are exceptions (especially in a pandemic!), but this is the kind of pattern most people follow, most days.

There are times and events in our life when our levels of original thinking will rise. When do you think that might be? Original thinking rises on holidays. We have new accommodation, new places to eat, new vistas, new adventures, new challenges and encounter new people. This feeling and exposure to newness creates new thinking. We also have elevated levels of new thoughts on bank holidays, weekends, birthdays and, to a certain extent, Christmas time – any time when our normal daily routine changes.

Our minds like new and interesting information, and can often feel starved of it. If you ask yourself at which stage in our life we learn the most information in the shortest space of time, it is during childhood. During this period, for example, we learn to walk, talk, read, write, expand our general knowledge, ride a bike, play sport, paint, play an instrument and many other subjects and activities. In adulthood, with much less new information being learnt on a day-to-day basis, we can find we are almost living on autopilot, except for when holidays or unusual activities break things up.

Questions

Earlier on I mentioned that your life quality can be influenced by the quality of your questions. What type of question might be heard from someone with a victim mentality? It could be along the lines of 'Why does it always happen to me?' Conversely a person with a positive attitude may look at a problem and ask, 'What can I learn from this?' or 'How can I be better next time?' I was speaking to someone recently who told me that a colleague of theirs will always question anything good that's happening in someone else's life. They will consistently pour scorn, prophesy doom and gloom and doubt anything positive happening around them. Were they born like this? Chances are, they probably developed a pessimistic lens through which to view life as a safeguard. They may also have a core question which dominates their life such as 'How can I prove that the world is a bad place?' So if they are ever faced with good news, their automatic reaction is one of negativity. Have you ever met anyone who, through past events, went on to acquire a negative attitude of fear and suspicion?

Exercise

Write down five questions that are empowering and five that are disempowering.

An example of an empowering question is 'How can I make the most of this morning?'

A disempowering question is 'Why me?'

Now spend some time noticing the disempowering questions that people (including yourself) may be asking.

When Things Go Wrong

It's only when something goes seriously wrong with this thinking process (or when we become aware of the fact that something is seriously wrong with it), that we start to view it as a system. We see that there's a Blueprint underpinning every thought, connection, presumption and idea. An invisible web, made up of your deepest-rooted ideas: those that have shaped your experience and become your truths.

Imagine your life is a car: you're in control, no-one else. I certainly can't take control for you. You have to do the work yourself. All I can do is to give you the tools within this book. You will need to try to really live them, to take on board the fact that mastery is acquired through repetition, and go with it. Eventually, you will replace your thinking habits with healthier, more productive and more functional ones. It's a question of perseverance, of putting your faith in the process, even if it feels unnatural at first.

Scenario 1

Mr and Mrs Williams have been invited to Mr Williams' company party. All partners are 'expected' at the gathering. Mr Williams loves parties, while Mrs Williams dreads these occasions. The party is happening two weeks' time, and already Mrs Williams is looking for excuses not to attend.

On the day of the party, Mr and Mrs Williams are both getting ready. Mr Williams is having a shower and starts thinking about the party. As someone who adores the chance to socialise, what sort of questions might he be asking himself about the party? He could be wondering, 'Who's attending?', 'Will there be free drinks?', 'Will there be music?', 'I wonder if I'll get to meet any of our colleagues from offices?' and 'Will it be another exciting late night?!' These are examples of upbeat, empowering questions which raise Mr Williams' mood whilst he's in the shower, as he visualises a great evening.

Mrs Williams enters the shower after Mr Williams has vacated it, and she too starts to think about the party. She starts to create disempowering questions at rapid speed. These include: 'Who's going to be there?', 'Will I know anyone?', 'Will anyone speak to me?', 'Will he flirt with anyone?', 'What time will we have to stay until?' and 'Will I be lonely again?' As Mrs Williams continues to ask negative, disempowering questions about the party, her anxiety slowly starts to build. She is now, as the popular phrase has it, working herself up into a state. By the time Mrs Williams has finished her shower, she is in an emotional state of heightened anxiety. The barrage of negatively focused thoughts has led to her feeling nervous and anxious.

The question you could ask is, 'Was Mrs Williams born with this fear of parties?' Logic and common sense would dictate: 'No'. Whatever has entered her Blueprint previously has now altered her perception of social events. It could be one of the following reasons:

- o She was embarrassed and humiliated at a previous party.
- o During childhood she felt all alone at parties.
- o When attending a wedding, her husband was overly flirty with another guest.
- o Since her teenage years, social situations have always made her feel anxious.

(It must be noted that in actual fact, it's not the social occasion itself which she was seeking to avoid, but the feeling or emotion that it evokes.)

When we examine the above example, it is quite clear that the type and quality of our future-focused questioning can have an immediate impact on our physiology.

Scenario 2

A man is attending an interview for a job that he is seemingly desperate to be offered. As he sits in the waiting area, he notices other candidates waiting for their interview. Immediately he starts to compare himself to the others. This is followed by worries and doubts about his capabilities to land the job on offer. Thoughts passing through his mind include, 'Am I good enough for this job?', 'Do I look OK?', 'What if they ask me questions that I don't know the answer to?', 'Have I wasted my time coming for the interview?

These people look so much better-dressed than me.' or 'What if I don't get the job – how am I going to pay the mortgage?' By the time the man enters the interview room, he too has worked himself up into an anxious state. This is compounded by his sweaty palms, a physiological by-product of the anxiety.

Our thoughts are being produced in the two primary parts of the human mind: the conscious and subconscious. Stop to consider for a moment what percentage of each is active in any given moment. To what extent is your subconscious mind dictating your thoughts, without you being aware of the fact? Most people understand that the subconscious mind holds a bigger sway than the conscious mind, but you might be shocked to hear just how dominant it is.

According to developmental biologist Bruce Lipton, along with numerous other experts, the evidence shows that most of the time around 95% of our brain activity is subconscious, sometimes even more than that. It's the subconscious mind that's running the show, dictating our cravings and desires, and the conscious mind only operates at a superficial level. While you sleep, you may think that your mind has switched off. This is not the case. Your subconscious mind is always active.

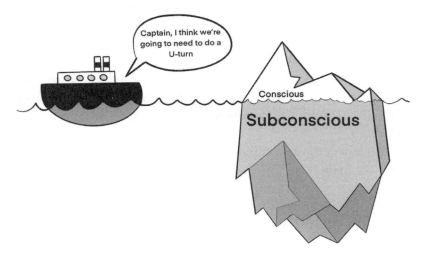

The conscious mind is only the tip of the iceberg. This is one fact that the experts agree on, although when it comes to a more in-depth understanding of the subconscious, there is still a certain amount of mystery and guesswork involved in our understanding of it. This is the case despite the fact that since Freud popularised the concept in the early twentieth century, numerous studies have been made of it, giving voice to a range of theories on the subject. Even today, amongst the psychotherapists, psychologists and the many other talking therapists who deal in the business of the mind's hinterland, there's a lot of debate about the subconscious. It is a rich and complex topic.

Unlike other aspects of psychology, which might relate to specific conditions, traits and personalities, though, the subconscious is relevant and fascinating for all of us. It is there, operating under the surface, and is shaping your behaviour constantly. Sometimes aspects of your personality might give an outsider a clue as to what might be going on in your invisible depths. The people closest to you may have a grasp on it, too, but generally we are unaware of one another's deepest selves.

In order to make changes at the deepest level, which is essential for fundamental behavioural transformation, it's no good appealing to the surface mind. For example, if you tell an anxious person to "chill out" or "be positive and you'll be fine", it doesn't help because it's only heard at a conscious level and doesn't resonate in a deeper way with their Blueprint. The person is also probably going to be highly irritated by you! An anxious person won't believe what you're saying because it hasn't entered the subconscious mind and in turn their Blueprint.

The power of the human mind is truly staggering when you stop to consider it. Your brain can perform an estimated ten quadrillion actions per second without you being aware of it. Your subconscious mind is a powerhouse, running all of your bodily functions and the vast majority of your thoughts.

But it also has a major fault: the subconscious finds it virtually impossible to distinguish between real events and thoughts. It experiences our thoughts about life as if they were real. In lab tests, scientists monitored athletes using muscle sensors, asking them to keep still but to imagine they were running or skiing. They observed that the same neural pathways in the brain fired signals as would fire if the athletes were exercising for real. This incredible phenomenon is a consequence of their neural pathways, which connect to the muscles, being readily activated by the power of visualisation.

At an even deeper level, what's going on in your subconscious mind creates an internal landscape that leads you to be drawn towards particular people and situations. The alarming thing about this is that if your subconscious is ruled by negativity, feelings of inadequacy, insecurity and low self-worth, the relationships and situations you find yourself drawn towards will be those that confirm your negative feelings.

The liberating and exciting flipside to this is that when you make deep shifts in letting go of some of what's going on underneath the surface for you, you will change your life, and the things you attract into it. This is a consequence of discovering a deep, unshakeable confidence in yourself.

Such confidence isn't to be confused with the sort that classic extroverts exhibit: of being smooth in company, adept at public speaking or assertive in meetings (although most of us might like to have more of these traits sometimes, too). We all know people who put a front on for other people. They create a mask that they show the world, but inside they are different people altogether. They may appear confident on the outside, but when you get to know them, they aren't really that confident after all. We've all heard people say, 'He seems so confident on the outside, but on the inside he's a mess,' or something similar.

What I'm referring to when I talk about a deep, unshakeable confidence is a deep sense of feeling at ease with and at peace with yourself. A sense of intrinsic worth that has nothing to do with status, success, accomplishment or the opinions of others. What you're striving for with the *Let It Go* process runs far deeper than external personality traits. It isn't fake or 'put on', and it's not something you 'show' to the outside world in any deliberate sense.

True confidence is being comfortable in your own skin. Some confident people are loud and outgoing, others are quieter and more reserved. That's a personality trait: it doesn't mean they aren't confident. Being confident has nothing to do with being loud or being noticed when you enter a room. The loudest person in the room is rarely the most confident. Confidence does not have a volume button.

Let's work backwards in the Blueprint model in order to understand the way we, and the people around us, behave.

A behaviour – say, shouting at your partner – is triggered by feelings (say, anger and fear) that are triggered by deep subconscious thoughts lodged in your Blueprint. This might be something along the lines of a deep-held belief that disagreements in relationships are dangerous as they can lead to abandonment. This is obviously one isolated example, plucked from an infinite variety of possible equivalents. At the root of all behaviour is your Blueprint.

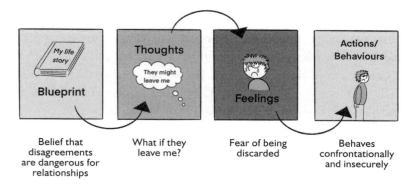

Blueprint	Thoughts	Feelings	Actions/Behaviours
Belief that disagreements are dangerous for relationships	What if they leave me?	Fear of being discarded	Behaves confrontationally and insecurely

Scenario 3

Two people in the workplace may look out of the window of the office. It's raining outside. The first person complains about how dreary the world is outside. The second person reframes the situation and although she admits that it's raining outside, she's so glad that she's inside and being paid to work as well!

In this situation, who's correct? There is no answer to that, as both people have valid opinions, yet differing attitudes towards the same set of circumstances. How anyone looks at a situation determines how they will respond or react.

Start looking at the way you think as a skill. It's not you, but a part of you, just like your body. It is something we never get trained in at school. It's true that we learn to absorb vast amounts of information there, but nobody ever teaches us how or what to think when the shit hits the fan. Please follow and practise the recommendations and tools found within this book, to give yourself the best chance of making a change.

University College London found in 2009 that it takes approximately 66 days for a new habit to form. Learning to undo decades of the way you think and replace it with a new way of thinking will take time, effort and persistence – oh, and patience!

Look at it like going to the gym. After time spent working out at the gym with a personal trainer, your body will change. After six months you notice you have increased strength, fitness and endurance. The mind is exactly the same. If you train it, you will eventually be in control of it, rather than it being in control of you. This all starts with a desire to change – a desire to let go of the unproductive habits and behaviours you are currently consciously aware of.

You will then:

- ✓ feel more confident
- ✓ feel more at ease with yourself
- ✓ trust yourself more
- ✓ value yourself
- ✓ believe in yourself
- ✓ take more risks
- ✓ not be easily offended
- ✓ stop criticising yourself
- ✓ reduce your negative thinking
- ✓ increase productivity
- ✓ change your habits
- ✓ be able to respond well when negative emotions and feelings arise.

5

React

'Be curious, not judgemental.'

~ Walt Whitman

As we have noted, the way we 'react' is at the very end of the Blueprint Process sequence described in Chapter 2. This automated psychological system creates the way we behave and react via our thoughts and feelings. Can you change how you react to pressure, stress or disappointment? The answer, I firmly believe, is 'Yes'.

I would like to highlight in this chapter that in certain situations, if we 'let go' instead of holding onto a negative thought or feeling, we are less likely to overreact. As we become more conscious of our ability to let go, and practise it, we start to understand ourself more deeply, as well as understanding others around us. The more we understand other people's behaviours, the greater our ability to let go of our own negative thoughts and emotions.

In this chapter I will illustrate how people 'react' in different situations, with common examples, some of which may be familiar to you. What I feel is really important to stress is that we never actually know what is going on behind the eyes of another human being. Only that person truly knows. We can form an opinion by paying attention to their reactions in a conversation, their micro facial movements and their body language, but this chapter will be exclusively focused on how and why people react, from a thinking and emotional viewpoint. Let me first offer you a few common reactions that people experience, through a series of questions. These are just food for thought.

- Have you ever met anyone who is oversensitive to being teased and cannot take a joke?
- Have you ever met anyone who reacted badly to criticism?
- Have you ever met anyone who snapped at something you said?
- Have you ever met someone who acted 'out of character' during a conversation? Perhaps even when, in concern, you asked them if there was something wrong, they continued to deny any problems, only for you to find out later that there had been an issue?
- Have you ever reacted angrily to a situation, originally thinking that someone had done you wrong, only to realise that you had made a mistake about the facts?
- Have you ever seen someone toot their car horn at another driver who had just cut them up on the road?
- Have you ever seen someone get into an argument with another person over a position in a supermarket queue?
- Have you ever seen anyone react negatively to another person's good news?
- Have you ever seen someone react negatively to someone challenging them over a fact?
- Do you know anyone who continually blames other people for their misfortune?
- How do you react to compliments?
- How do you react to criticism?
- How to do you react to someone being rude to you?
- How do you react to the feeling of being left out?
- How do you react to disappointment?
- How do you react to failing?

- How do you react to rejection?
- How do you react to someone appearing to put you down?
- How do you react to being ignored?
- How do you react to being treated unfairly?
- Have you ever had a bad day, and returned home only to snap verbally at your partner?
- Do you ever feel that you can react differently in different situations (in some situations you feel confident, while in other situations you can feel vulnerable, exposed and not good enough)?

Every day we go about our business, reacting to external stimuli from moment to moment. These include the weather, conversations with other people, our job, our family, events, social situations, stress, worry, uncertainty, certainty and our fears. The subject of how people react to such stimuli could fill an entire book, it's so important.

In order for you to let go of what could be holding you back in your life, getting to grips with the reactions of other people is key. Once you understand why others are reacting as they are, it's likely to lead you to several "Aha!" moments. This understanding will really help you to start letting go of something you currently believe to be true. Perhaps I could ask you a question:

What could you be thinking about yourself or someone else that might not be true? And if it isn't true, and you could let it go, would it result in you making a change in your life?

Awareness and Why It Is Crucial to Letting Go

Allow me to share a story with you, told to me years ago by a good friend of mine.

Lee and Erica had gone out for the evening – a rare date night – leaving the children with Erica's mum. As these evenings of 'parental freedom' were infrequent, there was almost a slight pressure for the evening to be perfect.

On this evening they had gone to an Italian restaurant they had not tried previously. It had, though, been recommended by good friends of theirs. The place was fully booked as it was Friday night, as well as the fact that the restaurant had recently been named the 'best restaurant' in their neighbourhood on TripAdvisor. Expectations were high.

As they were seated, Lee immediately noticed that the waiter had been abrupt to them. Erica hadn't really noticed as she was admiring the beautiful Italian decor of the restaurant. Lee decided to let the thought pass.

After waiting for ten minutes for service, Lee called the waiter over to order some drinks. He was met with a roll of the eyes from the waiter, which Erica also witnessed. Over the course of the next half hour, the couple then noticed the waiter systematically being rude to different tables. The service, they noted, was nowhere near the impeccable level for which the restaurant had been famed.

Lee and Erica started to become agitated as their first course had still not arrived. Again Lee called the waiter over and was told in a sharp voice that it would be along shortly, and to "have some patience". Lee was stunned by this comment.

At that moment, Erica noticed a very well-dressed man in a suit start to approach the tables around the restaurant. He appeared to be talking to the diners about something, though Erica couldn't hear what the man was saying. Within minutes, he finally arrived at their table and introduced himself as Franco, the owner of the restaurant. As Franco was about to continue speaking, Lee interjected and explained his huge annoyance at the behaviour of the waiter. He went on to say that it was the worst service that they had ever experienced, and that he was furious with the waiter for his impudence. Franco stepped back and, with his hands clasped together, asked politely if he could explain briefly what was happening. The couple nodded.

After apologising on behalf of the restaurant, Franco revealed that unfortunately Marco, the waiter, had lost his wife to cancer only two weeks previously. She had only been 31 years old. They had been childhood sweethearts and had two young children. Marco was supposed to be on compassionate leave for a month, but had insisted that he wanted to return to work earlier. After continued persistence, he had been allowed to come back into the restaurant, and this was only his second day back. He had now been sent home, and a replacement waitress had just arrived. Lee and Erica's mood changed instantaneously from one of anger to one of sorrow.

Often we can make an assumption and consequently judge someone, though we have only been afforded a split second to make that decision. It's human nature in action. However, if you look back over your life, how many times have you quickly judged a situation only for you to find out it wasn't what you thought it was? We never know exactly why a person is reacting as they are, but it would be useful to understand that it is a combination of what comprises their emotional Blueprint and current events that have directly impacted on their emotions. In this case, clearly Marco was devastated at what had happened to his wife and had possibly been experiencing many emotions, including anger and resentment. This cocktail of unwanted feelings unfortunately triggered him into his negative behaviour within the workplace.

Growing up, I would look at some people I knew and wonder how they could act so confidently in school and social situations. They always seemed to have everything go their way, whilst I always felt left out and insignificant. This inner dialogue led me to over-criticise myself and always react negatively to any praise or compliments which came my way. Situations would leave me frustrated, such as when I wanted to put my hand up in class to answer a question that a teacher had asked. I would always stop myself. This was for fear of answering incorrectly. I feared sounding stupid. I would then feel frustrated when the correct answer (my answer) was revealed by another person in my class. This led me to feeling less confident and having an overly self-conscious persona. I was unable to be assertive in any environment.

Looking back, it is clear that my primary focus was avoidance – avoidance of what I feared happening. We can often fear something happening, and will then engineer situations to ensure it doesn't materialise. When in your life have you avoided something which your gut was telling you was OK, but your head talked you out of? As a result, there was another missed opportunity.

When we learn to let go of what I term 'negative avoidance', our inner dialogue changes, and we start to listen to and trust our gut more often. We feel more confident in moving past self-limiting beliefs, irrational fears, doubts and uncertainty. The liberating feeling you experience allows you to react more positively in most situations.

Where Do Our Reactions Originate?

Our life is a series of events from the time we are born to the time we pass on. Each of these events happens to us, and we assign it a meaning. Think of it as placing a sticky note on a page of a book. Except this book is the story of our life. When we're in a similar situation later, we unconsciously refer back to this part of our 'story' and react according to what the sticky note says. If something has been given a sticky note with a negative message, we have a high chance of reacting negatively, and positively if the message is positive.

Reactions are born from experiences both in the distant past and also in the recent past.

The meaning that we assign to an event, past or present, when processed by our Blueprint generates thoughts which

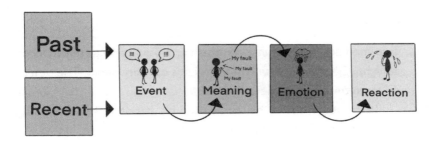

create an emotional reaction. This reaction is what the outside world observes, and judges us by. Sometimes we can consciously hide our reactions by faking an emotional response. Have you ever been in a particularly bad mood, but had to go into a social situation and conceal how you really feel? It can be arduous work, as you are consciously performing like an actor in that particular moment to display a façade of happiness.

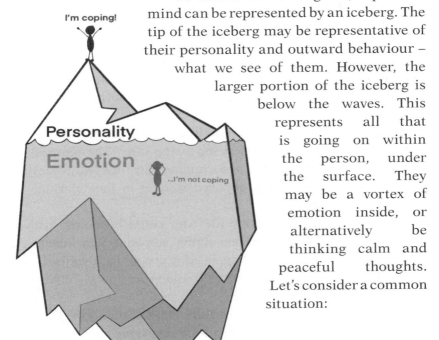

As shown in the diagram, a person's mind can be represented by an iceberg. The tip of the iceberg may be representative of their personality and outward behaviour – what we see of them. However, the larger portion of the iceberg is below the waves. This represents all that is going on within the person, under the surface. They may be a vortex of emotion inside, or alternatively be thinking calm and peaceful thoughts. Let's consider a common situation:

Scenario

Two men are involved in a car crash at a T-junction at ten o'clock at night. Clearly one man is at fault. Let's call him Henry. The other driver in this case will be called Jason.

Henry steps out of his car, raises his hands in honesty, and freely admits his 100% fault (responsibility) in the crash. He walks over to Jason's vehicle and immediately offers his driving details, including insurance papers, to Jason. The cars are slightly dented but completely roadworthy, leaving Henry confident that he should be able to get swiftly back home to his pregnant wife. However, Jason is absolutely livid. He furiously screams at Henry, gesticulating wildly, about why this accident has happened in the first place. Henry's honest explanation about driver error falls on deaf ears as Jason's voice bellows into the night sky.

In this situation, while Henry was focused on resolution and proceeding on home, Jason was focused on 'why' the accident happened. Clearly in this case, Jason was an angry man. This was the latest incident that had gone against Jason that day, and as a result had left him feeling that "life is against me". He was in fact reacting to how his day had gone, not just to this accident.

Sometimes people will react totally out of character because of the events they are experiencing at the time. The opinion that these things cause the, to formulate can then lead them to react in a diametrically opposed fashion to their normal response or reaction.

Think of someone in your life who could be doing just that. Maybe when you next encounter someone who reacts disproportionately to what's happened, you could ask yourself, "I wonder what's happening in their Blueprint that's causing them to react that way?"

From moment to moment, our life is a culmination of all the responses, reactions and resulting decisions that we are making. Think of any bad choices or decisions that you have made previously. It's not about going back and changing those decisions, as they are already in the past. It's more important how you react and choose from now on.

Some real-life examples from people that I have worked with are included towards the end of this chapter. When we learn to become consciously aware of how we are acting and reacting, we can immediately start observing our Blueprint and work out what beliefs about our self, core values or needs are required to change.

As well as our own reactions, we are consciously and unconsciously aware of other people's reactions to us. This can sometimes impact on our confidence. A very common method of gauging others' reactions is social media. We can post something on Facebook, Twitter, TikTok or Instagram, and patiently wait for the 'love'. Sometimes we have 72 likes for a post, which immediately feels like an outpouring of love towards us. Other times though, there can be an undeniably disappointing reaction to our post – one that we had expected to be popular. Consequently this can leave us feeling slightly disillusioned, with an accompanying dent in our self-confidence.

After the case studies, please complete the exercises. These are designed to assist you in making you aware of what you would love to let go of. Sometimes we are instinctively aware of what these are. More often than not, though, they have to be teased out of our subconscious mind.

Case studies

Laura

Laura attended a session after being told in no uncertain terms by her husband, "If you don't change your ways, it's going to lead to us breaking up." She was a top city lawyer working with a wealthy clientele for long hours.

It became clear during the initial session that Laura does not like to delegate. This particular behaviour has led her to overworking, under-delivering and placing a strain on her marriage.

At the session Laura thinks that it is something that she is born with – an inability to delegate. On closer questioning, I discovered that Laura had trust issues. She could not bring herself to trust others, and therefore had to do everything herself, as far as was humanly possible.

Laura's trust issues stemmed from her childhood and teenage years. One significant event was the failure of her parents' marriage, which had devastated her at the time. She remembered the feelings of being 'let down' by her parents. This had come after observing at school that other students' parents were still together, or were still friendly with each other. Her parents' divorce had been acrimonious, with Laura feeling exposed and at the mercy of future uncertainty.

Laura realised that she had to let go of this feeling of loss and uncertainty, which had led to her need to always be in control and not trust anyone.

This 'Aha!' moment came as complete surprise to Laura. She was relieved by the realisation that she could change, and that there was an origin to her destructive behaviour.

Laura felt that until she forgave her parents, the behaviour would still remain. She wrote a letter of forgiveness and understanding to both of her parents, and within a week started to feel a lot lighter and freer. Her father, who she hadn't been particularly close to, immediately called her and they met up for dinner.

Laura learnt that letting go through the power of forgiveness can be both liberating and enlightening, as you no longer waste your energy on the resentment or criticism of what happened in the past.

Laura has gone on to hire a PA, who she says she trusts with her life, and spends up to 30% more time with her family than before she started the letting go techniques. Hubby has called off plans for a divorce and the couple, I'm reliably informed, have never been happier!

Tony

I worked with a high-ranking policeman called Tony. In work and wearing the uniform, he was confident and very assertive in his ways. By contrast, out of the workplace, Tony suffered extremely low self-esteem. He often found it very difficult to interact socially, which would frustrate his wife, leaving her in tears after many arguments on returning home from friends' parties. Much to his dismay, Tony was also seen as "aloof" and "distant" by various family members.

During our face-to-face sessions, Tony admitted that he had always felt inadequate as a son while growing up. He had sought the love of his father, who seemed more intent on ridiculing Tony with sarcastic jibes and insults. The root cause of this behaviour was never discovered. However, it's clear that Tony's father was playing out the story of his own Blueprint.

The police uniform, for Tony, was a vehicle through which he could command respect and authority and which gave him a 'voice', as he put it. Unfortunately, the uniform could only afford him a temporary increase in self-esteem, when in the workplace. Tony would describe it as defensive armour against the outside world. He commented that he felt safe with its protection.

Tony's viewpoint on his father's behaviour began to change as he started to understand the Blueprint and its impact on how we think, feel and react. He became aware that his father must have experienced events and occasions which had shaped his own

Blueprint, and as a result had not treated Tony or his siblings with the fatherly love which they deserved.

Understanding a person's behaviour is not the same as condoning the behaviour. It is simply a mechanism which can help you to let go of hurtful and negative emotions that you may still be directing towards that person. I am sure you have seen or heard this following statement before:

Continually pouring scorn and resentment on someone is akin to you drinking cyanide and expecting the other person to die...

Yasmin

Yasmin attended the *Let It Go* programme. Her story:

For the first six years, Yasmin was happily married. She was confident and had a life that most women would envy. She was a doctor, her husband an engineer and they were blessed with two healthy children. Slowly over the years, though, her husband started to criticise her. If it wasn't the clothes that she wore, it was her hair, or her cooking. Over time, this caused Yasmin's normally buoyant confidence to diminish, though she would 'keep up an appearance' to the outside world, which she had learnt from how her mother had behaved while Yasmin was growing up. Eventually, after twenty years of marriage, Yasmin shocked the world she lived in and filed for a divorce.

The once-confident Yasmin was now a shell of her former self, having lost all her self-assurance by this point. What was interesting was how Yasmin now dealt with the outside world. She would no longer socialise and would repeatedly turn down requests for dates. She feared being put down by men, and no longer trusted them. Her top priority was her children. Yasmin admitted that she would say to herself that all men were controlling and selfish.

Following the divorce, Yasmin was made to feel guilty about it as her ex-husband had pleaded for a reconciliation, which she had refused. This left the children feeling a mixture of hurt and anger towards their mother.

Yasmin attended the *Let It Go* programme and freely admitted that she wanted a relationship, and that she was living in fear. Her primary fears, she disclosed, were fear of being let down, fear of the past repeating itself, and fear of failure.

Yasmin discovered that her Blueprint had changed over the course of her marriage and that her values, self-belief and fears had changed. As a result, she had viewed herself as a failure and had hidden behind her negative opinions of men in order to prevent herself from being hurt.

The emotions she now wanted to let go of were guilt, anger and the fears mentioned earlier. Yasmin felt that these emotions were not serving her, and were causing her to react to change very negatively, which was preventing her moving forward in her career and social life. She had been offered a senior hospital position but had turned it down because of her feelings of not being good enough, uncertainty about the future and the guilt that she needed to be home more with the children, who by now were 14 and 16 years old.

Yasmin worked relentlessly on her mindset to let go of the emotions which had impeded her life after the divorce. She will freely admit that life isn't perfect but also says that it is no longer a struggle. This, she says, was her breakthrough. For example, she no longer reacts to unwarranted comments made by family members about the divorce or its aftermath.

Tim

Previously Tim had worked in the building industry and had had a very well-paid job. He had got divorced 12 years before he attended the *Let It Go* programme. The divorce had hit him hard, and it had led him to being separated from his children for the entire 12 years. He would hide at the back of the sessions and would silently listen and absorb the information.

Growing up, Tim had watched his own single mother escape her emotional pains through the vehicles of drugs and alcohol. Tim's mother would regularly get drunk after arriving back home in the evening. This, Tim had noted, was his mother's default method of dealing with pain, and would later become his own choice of escape.

Tim had caught his then wife cheating with a family friend. This had devastated him. He took to excessive drinking as it was the only way he knew to cope with pain. He had rampaged at this family friend and had subsequently been arrested, but was released with no further action taken against him.

Unfortunately, the shame and anger that he started to feel immediately fuelled his drinking, which spilled into his work hours too. Within months, Tim was fired from his prestigious managerial post at the company where he had worked for nine years. This had then increased the anger, shame and alcohol binges.

Tim moved to another town to 'escape his demons', and fell into a depression. Dark thoughts consumed him daily, and he was subsequently put on a suicide watchlist by a local mental health organisation.

Following the *Let It Go* programme, he revealed to me that he had had extremely low expectations of any improvement in his confidence before attending the programme. But after a lot of hard graft with the tools I gave him, Tim returned to work within six months of the course.

He found himself no longer reacting badly to rejection or criticism, and would always now look forward to waking up and seeing what each day would bring. Whereas once upon a time he could be easily provoked into an argument, now he could let go of comments which would previously have affected him. In fact, he could now join in with some self-deprecation, which he admits he had never been good at doing!

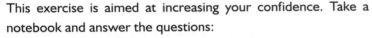

Exercise 1

This exercise is aimed at increasing your confidence. Take a notebook and answer the questions:

1. Does your confidence vary in different situations?
2. Which situations?
3. What happens to your confidence?
4. What are you thinking at the time?
5. How do you behave and react?
6. Who do you know who seems confident in these situations?
7. What do they do differently?
8. What thoughts do you think they are saying to themselves?
9. Could you speak to them frankly and openly for advice?
   Getting a different perspective and learning how it can help you think differently is priceless.

Exercise 2

The idea of this exercise is to help you become more aware of others around you. This way you may not become so affected by other people's negativity if it occurs.

Notice how people are 'reacting' around you.

Bear in mind that people's negative reactions are only a result of what we've discussed in this chapter. They are reacting to one of the following:

– an old story they still play out in their life
– a current challenge they are experiencing

Exercise 3

The aim of this exercise is to help you reduce overthinking and taking things personally.

Write the following on a post-it note, and put it somewhere where you will see it every day:

Everyone is on their own journey.

For me this was a lifesaver and game changer. It stopped me from taking things personally and gave me a licence to let go of the things people said or did which I would previously take personally, through being oversensitive.

TIP: Remember that everyone has a Blueprint which dictates how they react. We are only responsible for how <u>we</u> react, though. We cannot truly control others.

The minute that we realise this, it can be a very liberating experience. By realising that everyone is playing out their story from their Blueprint, it will give you the ability to pause and think, rather than react aimlessly.

6

The 'F' Word
(A Brief Introduction)

'There is no fear for one whose mind
is not filled with desires.'
~ Buddha

A man was starting a new job at a local printing company. He was both excited and nervous. He had left his old job after ten years of service, but thought that it was time for a new challenge.

On the way to work on the first day, the man crossed the busy road near his house and started to walk down the only street with direct access to his new place of work. As he walked along the street, he suddenly heard a growling noise behind him. He turned around to be confronted by a snarling rottweiler, frothing at the mouth. It started to bark loudly. Without hesitation, the man started to run down the street in the direction of his new company. The dog chased behind. The man reached the end of the street just in time, with the dog stopping abruptly just behind him, barking while it stood outside the last house on the street.

The man arrived in work, visibly shaken, sweating and slightly embarrassed at his own appearance. After his new colleagues had heard about the dog, they informed him that its bark was worse than its bite, so not to worry.

Unfortunately, the man stayed firm in his opinion that the dog was 'out to get him'. Every day for the next month, the man would be wary of the dog appearing. On some days it appeared and chased him down the street. On other days, much to his relief, it was nowhere to be seen.

However, due to his fear of the possibility of the dog being there, the man started to feel anxious first thing every morning. He started to wake up with sweaty palms and could also feel his heart racing.

One morning as the man walked down the street on the way to work, he suddenly saw the dog. Again it frothed saliva and started barking. Again, the man started to run as fast as he could. Suddenly the man stopped. In his mind, he screamed, 'Enough is enough!' He turned to face the dog angrily. The dog was stationary, ten yards away from him. The man promptly started to run towards the dog. He was suddenly both shocked and surprised. As he neared the dog, it opened its mouth to reveal something startling. The dog had no teeth!

Often we will give the emotion of fear teeth. We tend to run away from it, thinking that it is more harmful to us than it actually is. How many times in your life have you been scared of something happening, or not happening, and yet everything turned out well?

If you think again of your life as a car, the fuel in the fuel tank is your energy. What do you think the car's handbrake represents? This is a mechanism with which, in one sharp move, you can halt your progress immediately. It symbolises your fears. We have the capability to sabotage our own life by continually pulling on the handbrake, or letting our fears limit our potential.

It is believed that the little almond-sized amygdala, a small part of the brain, is linked to your fear responses. This emotional centre lights up when it detects perceived threats to your well-being, having evolved in caveman times as a mechanism for self-preservation and protection. Originally it developed to deal with external threats such as wild beasts entering the village, intruders entering your dwelling or the fear of being ostracised from your tribe. These days the amygdala creates fear signals related to modern problems such as overwhelm in the office or stress when boarding a flight. It is then the adrenal glands, secretors of adrenaline and a cocktail of other chemicals, which are involved with the physical reactions we experience when fear and anxiety strike.

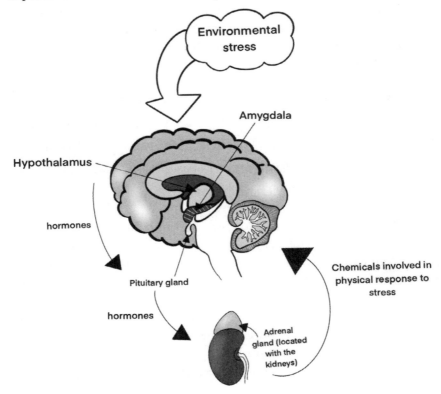

This whole pathway starts with our thinking. That's the bit that you can change: your thoughts.

Here are some more common examples of fearful reactions:

- You're are invited to a party and to get out of it, you decline by making excuses of not feeling well. This stems from fear of not knowing anyone at the party, which creates a secondary fear of being alone.

- You decide against applying for a new job for fear of not being good enough.
- You go on a third date and sabotage it by thinking, "It's not going to work out, so why bother?"
- You talk yourself out of doing things you want to do for fear of being hurt or rejected.

In all of these instances, you talk yourself out of the situation by yourself. No one forces you to make those decisions. The dialogue you have with yourself can determine whether you will take those risks or not.

 TIP: Remember, thinking is a series of questions and answers you have with yourself. If you ask yourself negative questions, then the outcome will be for your brain to try to protect you from getting hurt. Your fear of rejection, embarrassment and hurt will prevent you from moving forward.

It's plain to see that as a result, not only are you ducking out of potentially tricky emotions, you are also preventing yourself from experiencing all sorts of things that could bring you joy, satisfaction, challenge, purpose, achievement, intellectual stimulation, love, self-confidence and more.

Do you think that when you were born, you were born with fear of not being good enough? Were you born with the fear of being rejected or humiliated? Did you enter this world with fear of the future? Of course not. Something happened in your life to produce those fears.

I was travelling back from a workshop on a plane once. Sitting next to me in the aisle seat there was a very nervous passenger. As we talked, she confided to me that she had a fear of taking off, and of landing. Was she born like this? No, but the fear to her was real. It didn't stop her from flying, but it did make her feel very uncomfortable. For some people, such fear would stop them from flying all together, but she needed to fly due to her work commitments.

As we spoke, she started to describe her fear in detail to me: how it makes her heart race with anxiousness and her hands sweat. She hasn't consciously 'told' her body to behave in this way. It's an automatic reaction triggered by the activation of the fear from the amygdala.

I asked her what she thought the reason for the anxiety was, and she replied that she didn't know. The only thing she could feel at that moment was the feeling of not being in control. I asked her if she normally liked to be in control, to which she quickly replied, 'Always!'

When I asked her when the last time she felt that she was in control had been, she replied, "Never."

She went on to tell me that she vividly remembered her mother developing cancer many years earlier. As a child of 11 years of age, she had felt helpless as she watched her mother suffer. She had wanted to help her mum but didn't know how. She therefore felt helpless and powerless. This had left her feeling not in control of the situation.

In this woman's case, the feeling of not being in control at that tender age may have been a contributory factor, leaving her with a craving for a constant sense of control throughout her life. After that early traumatic experience, the 'need to feel in control' became part of her psychological Blueprint. This behaviour would run through her life, much a like a name running through a stick of seaside rock.

She doesn't get on the plane and consciously think, "I'm going to feel out of control today." However, her subconscious mind, the storehouse of her experiences and residence of her Blueprint, starts to create the major fear response.

There are hundreds of possible fears, but here are the most common ones. See how many you recognise:

- Fear of not being good enough
- Fear of dying
- Fear of being alone
- Fear of being ill

- Fear of being laughed at
- Fear of not having enough
- Fear of being poor
- Fear of being a failure
- Fear of the future
- Fear of the past repeating itself
- Fear of missing out
- Fear of being exposed
- Fear of being judged
- Fear of change

This list is not exhaustive!

The number one fear on the planet is of public speaking – for fear of being laughed at, fear of appearing stupid, fear of feeling exposed or fear of not being good enough. In one single activity, multiple fears stack up, one on top of the next.

We all have a fear of something and we pull on the handbrake in order to stop ourselves from moving forward in life. At their most extreme, some people's fears become so debilitating that they may even stop 'driving' altogether.

Fears keep you stuck. They send you back into a negative feedback loop where your Blueprint's most unhelpful and distorted preoccupations get reinforced. They don't serve you in any way.

The first step towards breaking through your fears is to take a long, honest look at what they are, and what's behind them. Not everyone is aware of what they fear until they stop to think about it. If you don't bring these fears to your conscious mind, they will stay under the surface in your subconscious and won't change.

Young children will tell you what they are scared of, as they are typically free, transparent and open. With us adults, it can be more difficult revealing what frightens us. Confessing that you are scared can be seen by some people as an admission of weakness. As most people would prefer not to appear weak, fears are often not discussed or addressed.

What I have witnessed through my work is that the same fears exist everywhere. Whether I'm working in New York or Helsinki, people are people, and have fears. Some people will label themself on social media as fearless, implying they have no fear. As you and I know, there is no such thing as 'fearless'. Fear is an ancient protective mechanism, as discussed. What we can agree on is that fearlessness is situational, not constant. You can feel fear in certain situations but not others. That is normal.

Look back at your life and catalogue the times that you were originally fearful, yet now no longer have that fear. You could be an accomplished home chef now, always entertaining people with dinner parties. Once upon a time though, the thought of entertaining would have filled you with dread! You could be an experienced traveller, whereas previously you were afraid to venture out of your own town. The list of your accomplishments in overcoming fears may be endless, however small each accomplishment may appear.

Exercise 1

On a post-it note, write the words: 'The dog has no teeth'. Place it where you can see it. This will remind you of the story above. We give fear teeth, when often it is undeserved and restrictive for our progress in life.

Exercise 2

Have a conversation with a trusted, non-judgmental friend, to discuss your fears. Often gaining a different perspective can assist in getting you unstuck. Write down what you learn from this conversation to gain even more clarity. Sometimes seeing it written down can stop the power of the fear over us.

Exercise 3

Write down in a notebook what thoughts you could be thinking to help create your fearful reaction. Ask yourself the question, 'What am I scared of?' or 'What am I scared of happening?' As it is our thoughts that create the fear, start questioning them.

Exercise 4

Take action in addressing a fear that you're currently feeling. By repeatedly meeting your fear head on by taking action (like moving towards the dog with no teeth), your fear will start to diminish.

For example, it could be:

- phoning your boss to ask for that long-overdue pay rise (fearing rejection and humiliation)
- going to the gym even though you are convinced people will think you are fat (fearing being laughed at)
- telling your mum and dad that you are emigrating (fearing upsetting them)

After you have completed this action, write down how you feel in your notebook.

Exercise 5

Write down things that you used to be scared of, but which now no longer concern you. How does this knowledge make you feel?

7

The 'Stick of Rock'

'At the centre of your being, you have the answer;
you know who you are and you know what you want.'

~ Lao Tzu

Imagine a stick of seaside rock – the type you find at the fairground or at a seaside resort. Now imagine at one end you see the word 'Blackpool'. You look at the other end and you see the same thing: 'Blackpool'. You notice that if you were to cut through the rock at any point, you would always see the word 'Blackpool' as it runs all the way through the centre of the rock.

Now imagine that we have certain negative habits and behaviours which run similarly through our life. This thread of negativity therefore impacts on our entire being, as it is ever-present. Here are certain examples of these behaviours which you may or may not be aware of in yourself.

- Blaming
- Criticising
- People-pleasing
- Negative attitude to life
- Mistrusting
- Feeling hard done by ("Life is unfair")
- Victim identity
- Irresponsibility (not caring of consequences of actions)
- Always saying "I should…" ("I should lose weight", "I should change my job")
- Always devaluing yourself/putting yourself down
- Always comparing yourself negatively with others
- Always focusing on worst-case scenarios
- Never finishing things
- Oversensitivity
- Overconcern with status
- Overconcern with what others think
- Overanalysing
- Refusing to let things drop
- Deep-seated fear (e.g. including fear of failure, fear of disappointing others, fear of abandonment, fear of the past reoccurring, fear of the future, fear of being alone, fear of not being liked, fear of being judged)

What behaviour or emotion could be running through your life which manifests itself in every area, like the name in your own stick of rock? The likelihood is that you formed this at some earlier point in your life. You don't really need to know when or how. A powerful realisation would be to acknowledge that it exists and that you'd like to let it go.

 TIP: It might be worth asking a trusted person what negative behaviour you keep demonstrating.

Allow me to offer you some examples:

82

Case studies

Carol

Carol is a procrastinator. She puts everything off. Her favourite phrases are "I'll do it later", "Let me think about it", and "I'm not sure whether to or not." As a consequence, Carol often complains at her lack of progress in her business, and also about how tasks seem to take her twice as long as other people. She bemoans her 'bad luck' and says, "Perhaps I shouldn't be in business," without being fully aware of her underlying bad habit. As a result, this is costing her customers and subsequently profits. So why is Carol putting everything off, and delaying taking action? There could be numerous reasons, including fear of not being good enough, fear of failure or the need to stay within her comfort zone (implying a fear of the unknown).

Hence Carol's stick of rock includes procrastination.

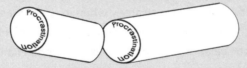

Greg

Back in 2013, Greg attended coaching sessions because he felt depressed, confused and frustrated. These emotions were mainly confined to the area of his romantic relationships. The relationships would start off well, with several months of what appeared to be a blissful romance. Then for no apparent reason, the relationship would fail around the six-month mark. This would leave Greg feeling like a failure. No matter how much he analysed and pondered the demise of the latest relationship, Greg could not fathom what the underlying reasons were.

During one of the sessions we discussed his daily morning rituals. Greg started to talk about his routine, and mentioned something quite startling. He would play music every morning. This in itself is nothing out of the ordinary, but the type of music was quite interesting. Greg, on waking up every day, would listen to love songs. Songs by Whitney Houston such as 'Didn't We Almost Have It All', 'I Get So Emotional' and 'The Greatest Love of All' would blare out of his speakers. These songs, Greg revealed, were favourites he and his ex had loved. Their relationship had ended over ten years earlier, but Greg was reluctant to let go of the 'good times' as he reminisced about his 'first love'.

Greg had experienced severe emotional pain in the form of feelings of rejection and disappointment over the break-up. This had left him feeling devastated and eventually angry. His ex-partner had left him for another man, which had left Greg with the belief that women are not to be trusted and "will cause you pain if you let your guard down".

As we continued the sessions, it became apparent that Greg had developed a protective strategy when in a relationship. This would take the form of him sabotaging things himself. He would ensure that the relationship would fail by his mood changes, lack of communication and persistent need for reassurances from his partner. By doing this, Greg would preserve his need to avoid pain and keep himself in control of his life.

As any new relationship approached the six-month mark, he would start to feel "vulnerable and exposed" – the same feelings he had experienced at the end of the relationship ten years earlier. Greg was trying to avoid those feelings, and so would ensure that each subsequent relationship would fail. He would not return his girlfriend's calls, would show up late to meet her and became tight with money on dates, when previously he had been generous. Eventually each girlfriend would be forced to throw in the towel after losing patience with Greg's behaviour.

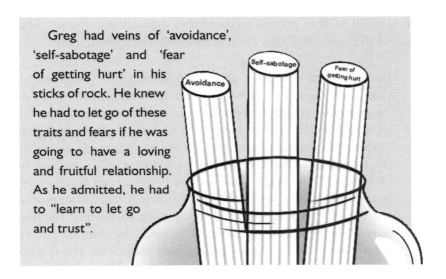

Greg had veins of 'avoidance', 'self-sabotage' and 'fear of getting hurt' in his sticks of rock. He knew he had to let go of these traits and fears if he was going to have a loving and fruitful relationship. As he admitted, he had to "learn to let go and trust".

Often experiences that we've had in our life result in us trying to protect ourself and keep ourself safe. In Greg's case, he was trying to stop history repeating itself and to avoid the feelings which had caused his life to fall apart previously. As human beings, naturally we will often try and avoid letting situations happen which have caused us so much pain in the past.

What is running through your rock? What behaviours do you think you are continually playing out which impede your progress in your career and relationships? Is there something you keep doing that stops you living the life you would like, but you can't seem to help yourself? Would you say it is time let this go? What will be the cost to you if you don't let it go? What has it cost you so far, and what will it cost you in the future?

As we can have more than one stick of rock, we can also have more than one unproductive behaviour which we are engaging in. Imagine that someone is always trying to get the last word in an argument or discussion. What does this say about them? It could mean that they need to feel significant. This means that they are feeling insignificant inside, and by getting the last word in, this 'proves' to them that they are significant. The word that goes through their rock could be 'significance'.

> Imagine that you meet up with a friend and you mention that you're going to New York for a minibreak. Instead of them feeling openly happy for you, they take great pleasure in telling you that they have been to New York three times! Do you know anyone like this? Whatever you seem to say or do, they've done more or better. It's not that they want you to feel bad, it's that they want to feel better about themselves. Something in the past has made them feel insignificant and now, as a result, they consistently look to be feeding that part of them that feels depleted. It could be that they were one of three children growing up, and always felt left out, or perceived themself to be different to the other two siblings, and therefore felt unloved.

Whatever happens to us in our childhood impacts our emotional Blueprint. As a result, we then develop a particular way of thinking and feeling that is unique to us. Our self-confidence and self-esteem (or lack of!) develop during this time.

Any behaviour that you're currently not proud of is a result of something from the past. Something may have happened that you can't even remember, but which caused you to form a set of beliefs, values and opinions which run your life. Being aware of these behaviours can be a giant step for your personal growth. If we are not aware of how we are behaving, then we simply cannot change it.

The following exercise is designed to expose any faulty thinking and behaviour which could ultimately stop you from changing your life. Whether you are thinking that you need to change one small aspect of your life or your entire life, this is the same process. You are only looking to uncover what you would like to let go of.

Exercise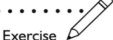

Take a pen and a notebook and answer the following questions as honestly as possible.

1. What behaviour do you continually exhibit that frustrates you? You may have more than one stick of rock in your psychological background. (Revisit the list at the beginning of this chapter for common issues.)
2. How long have you been doing it?
3. What has it cost you?
4. What negative qualities do you see in yourself that you're not proud of?
5. Are you finally willing to change them by the process of letting go?
6. What positive and helpful behaviour would you like to replace them with?

8

The Toxic Thinking Trap and How to Escape It

'Don't find fault, find a remedy.'
~ Henry Ford

We've talked a lot about the impact of introducing positive mental habits. In this chapter, I want to look at the impact of facing up to your negative default behaviours, which I like to bundle together and call your 'toxic thinking'.

Scenario

You spend 30 minutes with a friend over a cup of coffee, and for the entire time they blame, complain, judge and criticise the world. They blame the weather, complain about their wife and even criticise their colleagues. How do you feel? Drained and fairly exhausted, I'm sure.

Two weeks later you see this person in the supermarket and decide to jump into the next aisle. Why is that? You don't dislike them. However, you disliked how they made you feel. You have no intention of allowing them to drain your energy again on this particular day!

The disempowering collection of thinking and unproductive habits often seen in toxic thinking include blaming, complaining, judging, criticism, expectations, assumptions and always wanting to be correct.

The next time you're around anyone who is engaged relentlessly in any of the above, notice their energy. You'll notice that it's negative. This energy is completely the opposite of the energy of an empowering and energising person you may know.

The toxic thinking described is the negative mental reflexes that kick in whenever you're under pressure or feeling threatened. They are likely to be so deeply embedded in your thinking that you may not even be aware of their influence on the way you perceive the world.

The particulars of these are likely to be unique to you, and will have been informed by the psychological cocktail of influences you've experienced. For most of us, these defaults are introduced in childhood, picked up by observing the reactions and behaviours of the adults around us. So if your parents or other significant adults in your life had strong negative tendencies, which you were drip-fed throughout childhood, it will colour your perception of everything in your world. The toxic chatter also develops as we experience unpleasant life events, e.g. divorce, watch the daily news and become embroiled in conversations with friends, colleagues and family.

The reason it's so important to disrupt and challenge these negative paradigms is that they are working against you. They sabotage your ability to take responsibility for your life and define it on your own terms.

Every time you blame, complain, judge, expect, criticise or assume, you're giving away your personal power. In this voluntary act of self-sabotage, you undermine your own control and clarity in any given situation. These negative attributes can be influenced by anger, frustration, feeling threatened and feeling stuck in life.

Let's look at an example.

Case study

Sandra

Sandra came to see me because she couldn't seem to find employment in her field of work. On paper, she had an impressive CV. She had, however, taken time out to have children. Unfortunately, through no fault of her own, she had been made redundant from her job in marketing shortly after returning from maternity leave. This had dented her confidence immensely, leaving her feeling anxious and frustrated.

Sandra was hit by paralysing waves of self-doubt every time she attended a job interview. Her head was constantly filled with self-criticism. She assumed she would be 'too old' and 'out of the loop' to be appealing to an employer. She complained regularly to family and friends about being consigned to the 'scrap heap of life'. Sandra sadly blamed her former employer for all of her emotions and her predicament at the time. Her vitriol towards her former boss consumed a considerable amount of energy, even though she hadn't worked there for a few years.

Here are a few examples of the types of thing Sandra said when she came to see me:

- 'People always take me for granted.'
- 'I'm my own worst enemy.'
- 'Technology moves so fast that all my experience is out of date...'
- 'I'm too frumpy and mumsy now to work in media.'

The negative vocabulary that Sandra consistently employed in conversations with people caused her to sabotage any progress that she could have made. The automated toxic chatter meant that even at interviews, she would betray herself in the view of potential employers. This demeanour of self-doubt, worry and negativity would always be detected by interviewers, leading to unsuccessful results.

When attending interviews, Sandra would silently blame her former employer and herself and would extend the negativity to potential new employers. She had begun assuming that they would 'write her off' even before the interview had started.

Looking at this situation from one point of view, this sort of pessimistic thinking might seem like a form of self-preservation: assume the worst and you won't be disappointed. But it's actually the opposite – a sure-fire way to stay stuck. It gives a certain amount of relief in the moment as it offloads blame, steering it away from you and projecting responsibility elsewhere: another person, a situation, bad luck – whatever. But it offers no satisfaction as it casts you as a powerless victim.

Sandra completed my course and began to practise what I taught her (and will teach you as the book progresses). It felt alien to her at first, and she reported feeling self-conscious and false in the beginning. But within a few weeks, she reported feeling more positive. Sandra also started to engage more with the Attitude of Gratitude, which we will look at later, and reported how differently she now viewed life. Little things like being able to walk outside in fresh air now felt more important to her than the negative blame strategy that had consumed her until this point.

She decided to stop writing herself off in her conversations and consciously choose more hopeful, positive language when she talked about herself. She signed up for a course on social media to bring her skills up to date. She identified the friends and family members who were most likely to draw out her own negativity and she avoided them. [I'm often asked what to do about family, as you can't eradicate them from your life! My respectful suggestion is to minimise the time you spend with people who are likely to increase your negativity. A very useful strategy to root out negative influences in your life is described later in the book – keep reading!]

Over a three-month period of consistent reflection and practising letting go of the dominant toxic chatter, Sandra re-entered employment. Much to her delight, she was offered a job in marketing within the media world. She is convinced that this opportunity would not have been presented to her if she had not retrained her mindset and inner emotional responses.

Sandra readily admits that she still has to remind herself to use positive language and not to overshare her negative feelings about herself in company, but she acknowledges that she has made incredible progress.

Let's take a look at the times when your toxic thinking is most likely to kick in:

- **When you're feeling under pressure**
  Perhaps you've been asked to give a big presentation at work, or you have a job interview. The weight of other people's expectations can trigger a sense of imposter syndrome and a terror of feeling exposed.
- **When you feel slighted**
  Attaching disproportionate negative significance to something harmless (say a friend not replying to a text message) can trigger a spiral of negative self-talk.
- **When you feel overwhelmed**
  Particularly if you suffer from low-level anxiety, being faced with a lot of stimulation at once – whether it's a large group of people at a party or somebody else's angry mood – can trigger overwhelm. We can feel overwhelm in the workplace or in situations such as having to look after an elderly family member while the rest of the family offer no help.

- **When you feel vulnerable**
  Situations where we're physically or emotionally vulnerable (pregnancy and labour, illness, the end of a relationship, moving to a new town) can send your toxic thinking settings into overdrive.
- **When you are feeling threatened**
  You may be deep in a conversation with someone where you feel threatened by what that person is saying. It may not be that person's intention to leave you feeling that way, but you have interpreted it as such.

How Do We Identify Our Toxic Thoughts?

To identify your own patterns, you'll need to take an honest look at the workings of your thought process. Here's an exercise to help you.

Exercise 1

Take a pen and paper and make a note of your own toxic-thinking settings. To get you started, try answering the following questions:

1. Who are you most likely to blame when things don't go well for you? Yourself? Your parents? Your partner? Your friends? Your colleagues?

2. What negative behaviours do you notice yourself repeating? Write a long list and review it. For example do you blame, complain, judge, criticise, act resentful or always want to have the last word?

3. What negative myths and 'facts' about yourself do you accept? These could be things like: 'I'm disorganised', 'I can't handle confrontation', 'I'll always be an outsider', 'I'm not good around groups of people', 'I'm not a practical person', 'I don't make friends easily'. Be ruthless and honest and make a note of them all.

4. Finally answer this: What behaviour do you excel in that you wish you didn't? It might be putting everyone else first, or being pessimistic. Are you guilty of people-pleasing, procrastinating, perfectionism or starting things but never finishing them? How much does this frustrate you? What would happen if you let it go?

5. Do you join in conversations with negative people to feel good about yourself?

It may be quite a shock to see all this written down. Many people find that they hadn't been conscious of the fact that they hold negative opinions of themselves, even though these thoughts have been effectively ruling their lives up until now. But recognising the dysfunctional features of your thought pattern is often the first step on the path to resetting your mindset.

Exercise 2

Find a rubber band and put it on your wrist.

Once you've identified your toxic defaults, the next challenge is to catch yourself blaming, complaining, criticising, assuming, expecting and judging. Your objective is to notice this type of thinking from moment to moment and combat it. Remember, awareness will build confidence. One way to do this is to create a physical trigger that will help you to mark these thoughts and remind you that they are harmful: Try pinging your rubber band, or pinching your hand hard enough to feel a bit of pain. Every time you catch yourself having a toxic thought, snap the elastic band or pinch your hand. You give your mind a telling-off and your body feels the physical side of the 'ping'. It will help your resolve to break the habit, reinforcing the sense that this thinking is doing you damage and needs to be replaced with something positive that serves you better. You are effectively bringing your toxic thoughts to the surface.

The link between your physical and emotional reactions is obvious. When you feel nervous, you sweat and your heart beats faster. When you're happy, you smile and your eyes radiate. When you're feeling low, your posture closes up, your shoulders slump and your gaze drops. So creating a physical anchor that helps you to 'feel' bad thinking when it takes hold has a deep resonance, tapping into the deep interconnectedness of your body and mind.

This powerful process of associating pain with toxic thinking raises awareness and is a reminder for you to let it go. Clients tell me that they'll find themselves thinking, "I used to be like that," as they listen to a colleague or family member blaming, complaining and judging others. Within weeks of listening to the toxic thoughts of others around you, you will feel a heightened sense of awareness. Some people have mentioned to me that it's akin to feeling awake for the first time in their life. That's personally very profound to hear.

 TIP: Make sure you invest in those elastic bands!

Often, this part of the *Let It Go* philosophy also enables clients to identify exactly where their blame/complain behaviour started. It enables them to see with renewed clarity how blame/complain modes operate within their family. Once you begin to recognise these patterns, you spot them everywhere.

Attuning yourself to blame/complain thinking will increase not only your level of self-awareness but your awareness of others. You'll develop the ability to see through low-level whingeing and negativity to the dysfunctional toxic-thinking system that underpins it, and you'll feel yourself consciously moving away from it.

After developing an awareness of toxic thinking through their work with me, some clients have distanced themselves from friends that they have had for years, purely because they see the extent of their negativity clearly for the first time and recognise that being around a particular person has a draining effect on them.

Here are a couple of everyday examples of common negative thoughts that can be triggered by the most seemingly insignificant catalyst.

1. The tumbleweed text

Emma sends Sarah a text message asking her if she wants to go for a drink later that night. Sarah takes quite a long time to respond to her.

Emma thinks, 'I wonder if she's in a bad mood with me? Perhaps I've done something to offend her? Why is it that I'm always the one to make the effort with friends?'

She blames herself and allows anxiety to fabricate a host of reasons why Sarah hasn't responded. She is also assuming the facts before being aware at all of the truth. (In reality, Sarah has just had a really busy, stressful day, and got stuck in a long meeting. It has nothing to do with Emma.)

2. The thankless driver

Mick is driving home. He's stressed about work and keen to see his kids before they go to bed, and the traffic is terrible. The traffic is crawling along and there is a car waiting at a crossroads trying to edge out, but nobody is stopping to let it join the stream of traffic. Mick slows to a stop and lets the car out, but the driver doesn't say thank you. No lights, no friendly hand gesture, nothing. Mick is suddenly and overwhelmingly furious. He swears under his breath. He is disgusted by the ungraciousness and thoughtlessness of the other driver. It triggers a series of dismissive assumptions about the driver in his head. He's a selfish idiot who has no concern for other people. Not only that, he's typical of drivers now: 'It's every man for himself on the road nowadays,' he says to his wife later that evening.

Acknowledging the fact that imagined slights generally have none of the significance we attach to them can be really freeing. It's a helpful reminder that our toxic thinking endows us with a false sense of negative significance. In reality, the majority of the time, nobody is thinking about you, what you've done wrong, or your behaviour at all. They have their own stuff going on and they're caught up in that.

When you're aware of the faulty nature of this type of thinking and you realise it's happening, you're gentler on yourself and others.

Many of us are good at blaming ourselves, but this isn't the same thing as taking responsibility. It's passive and retrospective and therefore totally pointless. In contrast, taking responsibility for your part in something that has happened (or in the case of patterns in your life, keeps happening), is active and empowering. A sense of responsibility helps you to take ownership of the things you can do to change yourself, by altering your attitude and resetting your Blueprint.

We can self-limit by complaining that we always attract a certain type of person or relationship: 'Men always cheat on me,' we might say, or 'I always end up with overbearing partners.' But the truth is, we have the potential to attract all sorts of people into our lives, it's just that we only let particular people in (those that we think we 'deserve' at a deep psychological level). These people may well treat us in a consistently disrespectful, negative and thoughtless way, but that's because we've conditioned ourselves to expect that as a consequence of deep internal narratives that are likely to be the result of a bad experience in our formative years.

On the flipside, when you're aware of your blame/complain tendencies and consciously seek to quiet them within yourself, choosing to privilege positive, self-bolstering thoughts that serve you better, you develop what the entrepreneur Warren Buffet calls a strong 'inner scorecard' – a personal value system that exists in spite of anything other people might think. This is a hallmark of integrity and liberates you from the tyranny of people-pleasing, and from the guilt-tinged 'ought to' and 'should have's that so often lead us to act in ways that go against our instincts or deepest desires.

When we're able to do this, the sky is the limit. Let me tell you a little story to demonstrate the power of a strong inner scorecard.

Back in the 1970s, a man was learning to play the guitar and sing. He was playing in bars in New York and New Jersey. He loved music, but his family thought it was just a hobby. He went from bar to bar and busked in the streets, trying to get a record deal without any luck. One day he met his idol, Bruce Springsteen, who said that his performance was OK, but in his opinion the man should stick to his day job as Springsteen didn't think he was going to make it. Naturally, this was not what the man wanted to hear from someone who was a great musical influence in his life.

If he had listened to his idol, we would never have heard of Jon Bon Jovi. If he had accepted Springsteen's criticism as the truth, then he wouldn't have gone on to be as successful as he has been. He had a strong inner scorecard, so he was able to listen to what his idol had to say and disregard it, understanding that it was just an opinion and not the truth.

In contrast, somebody with low self-esteem will take any criticism on board and internalise it. They may take criticism really badly in their romantic relationships too, feeling every negative comment doubly. This could leave them frozen and fearful, with deep insecurities.

The knock-on benefits of letting go of your toxic thinking defaults are really powerful. I've seen some incredible examples amongst the people I've worked with.

Case studies

Jessica

One lady I saw was a mother of two primary school-aged children. Mornings were a painful battle that culminated in her screaming at the kids, who weren't listening to her, and often ended in tears. She felt like she was failing as a mother, but also that she had children who were unusually uncooperative and moody. After learning the *Let It Go* tools and continually practising them, she found a new sense of calm. She changed the way she communicated with the children.

She dropped her voice instead of raising it, got down on their level, looked them in the eye and explained what she needed them to do. She was starting to act from a place of calmness. The mornings became smoother and less stressful for everyone. 'I don't blame, complain, moan and bitch at them and about them any more. I was giving out so much negative energy,' she said to me. 'They were picking up on it and it was impacting on everybody's mood. When you expect the worst, you get it. Now, because I'm calm, they're calm.'

Gareth

Another client came to me feeling stuck in his career. He kept being overlooked for promotions and, despite his experience and competence, felt sidelined and frustrated in his job. But when he begain to think about his toxic thinking settings, he realised that he was the voice of doom in the office. He'd never realised this before, but he'd earned a reputation as the person who would pour scorn on new plans, point out the problem with everything and put himself forward as the voice of 'reason' in group brainstorms. He was well liked, but known as a naysayer and a cynic.

It came as a real surprise to him when he recognised that his pessimism was colouring other people's perception of him, and creating a negative overall impression. It was tough for him to retrain himself to curb these tendencies, but when he did, the pay-off was transformative. He was promoted within six months – and better than that, he felt significantly happier both inside and outside of work as a result of his new, more positive mindset. His relationships within his workplace also started to change as colleagues now found him more approachable and likeable.

The challenge to yourself now is to go deep and to root out the toxic thinking, beliefs and strategies that you involve yourself in – which, as you can see, are obstacles blocking your way to a happier life.

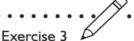

Exercise 3

A particularly powerful exercise, not for the faint-hearted, is to ask 3–5 of your most trusted friends to give you some feedback, based on their observations of how you appear to speak and act in front of them. As our toxic thinking is often spoken on autopilot, we are often surprisingly unaware of its presence in our everyday conversations. Your friends can often be invaluable in assisting you in identifying it. Awareness is, after all, the first step to letting go.

Naturally, you may at first hesitate to do this exercise as no-one likes hearing what they feel to be criticism. If you could view this exercise as a fantastic opportunity to start moving towards the best version of you, I have found that it really helps. It will be a difficult exercise, but one where the feedback can really help improve your future life, happiness and success. Your friends may feel uncomfortable about doing this – reassure them that this is for your benefit and that you won't hold what they say against them. But you'll need to mean that!

Exercise 4

When you're having a conversation with a group of friends who are willing to participate, record it. Then play it back. This will illustrate to you how you interact in social situations and what type of vocabulary you are currently using. You will quickly ascertain whether you tend to blame, complain or judge, and in what proportions.

Exercise 5

There may be instances in conversations where you know you are correct factually, but another person insisting they are correct leaves you feeling frustrated or deflated. Whatever the reasons for the other person's stubbornness, just saying the following words is a very powerful emotional diffuser, as the words are mutually beneficial to both parties.

'We'll agree to disagree.'

Awareness and clarity

Can you remember when you saw yourself speak on film for the first time? To many people this can be a strange feeling, and there's a good chance that what you heard and saw in the video didn't fit with the self-image that you had stored internally. In other words: you were shocked and surprised at how you looked and sounded!

It is my hope that through the exercises above, you will become acutely aware of your toxic thoughts and see the enormous potential benefit of letting them go one by one. This feeling of empowerment can be enhanced by your growing awareness of other people's toxic thinking and habits.

9

Can You Teach an Old Dog New Tricks?

'The chief function of the body is to carry the brain around.'
~ Thomas A Edison

One popular misconception which has been passed down through generations is the belief that 'You can't teach an old dog new tricks.' The idea behind this is that as you advance in age over the years, your mental ability to learn new skills and adopt new beliefs erodes. However, scientists have found this to be untrue, with the exciting relatively new science of neuroplasticity (where *neuro* denotes brain nerve cell, while *plasticity* refers to adaptability).

Scientists have discovered that the brain is actually very responsive to change, and changes at the brain-cell level. Hence a 75-year-old woman can potentially learn to speak Italian, play the violin or develop graphic design skills.

It is fascinating that the 3 lb master computer we possess, with 100 billion neurons (brain cells) forming millions of inter-neuronal connections, adapts and responds to the world around it with such elegance and ease. It has now been found to have the ability to rewire itself, and not only that. Research has found that through the process of neurogenesis, we are able to grow new brain cells. This can potentially happen at any stage of your life.

The brain can grow new cells through periods of learning and memory, and physical changes to the brain, e.g. stroke. Hence people who have been injured or suffered a stroke have successfully learnt to walk again, as the brain rewires itself. This occurs when the person repeatedly stimulates brain cells by repetitive thoughts, emotions and actions. Like building a muscle through repeated actions, the brain's neural pathways start to strengthen, with links between different brain cells deepening in physicality. As a result, we literally become what we constantly think and do daily.

It is reported through the work of K Anders Ericsson, Professor of Psychology at Florida State University, that it takes approximately 10,000 hours of deliberate and purposeful practice to become an expert at a skill. If you think back to anything you have ever mastered in your life, including walking, talking and writing, it was achieved through the process of repetition.

As we repeat new thoughts and actions, these eventually form new habits. These habits become automated within our daily life at brain level. Put it this way: every time you learn a new skill, you will eventually, by repetition, create a new brain pathway dedicated to that skill. The stronger the brain pathway, the more effective the skill and the less you have to think about it.

When you first learnt to drive, everything was carried out at the conscious level. You had to 'think' and repeat to learn the complex process of driving. Have you ever seen a learner driver's face? It is the epitome of focus and concentration, as they are deep in the process of deliberately practising new thoughts and behaviours.

Now fast-forward to five years after they have passed their driving test. They are no longer consciously thinking about what pedals to press or how to react as they come to a set of traffic lights. This skill has been passed over to the subconscious mind for automated processing.

Science has shown that that the brain links up different areas concerned with body movement, coordination, balance, memory and judgement, so that we rarely have to think consciously again about the driving process. Hence if someone does not drive a car for almost a decade and then wants to return to driving, they only have to spend a comparatively short amount of time practising again to become confident behind the wheel.

A famous study demonstrating the brain's ability to change was published by neuroscientist Eleanor Maguire of University College London in 2011. Maguire studied the effects of studying for the Knowledge Exam on trainee London Black Cab drivers In order to pass this test, they have to master no fewer than 320 basic routes and all of the 25,000+ streets, as well as approximately 20,000 landmarks and places of interest in London. This is achieved by traversing the streets of the city over a three- to four-year period, usually on a moped.

Maguire and her colleagues followed the journey of 79 would-be London cab drivers over four years, regularly taking measurements of certain areas of the subject's brain using MRI (magnetic resonance imaging) scans. As a control group, Maguire also measured the brains of 31 non-taxi drivers of similar age, intelligence and education, and with similar short- and long-term memory skills at the beginning of the study. The study was interested in what happens to the brain when you have prolonged intense focus on spatial awareness.

What the results indicated was that the hippocampus, the area of the brain involved in the memory of maps, streets and the location of buildings and landmarks, and without which you would not know how to get home, had grown significantly in the successful trainee cab drivers. This was in comparison to the control group, which showed no significant increase in the hippocampus.

The study demonstrates that by repetitive input through the senses, thoughts, feelings and actions, we have the ability to create new neural networks in the brain. This, then, is proof that by repetitive thinking, your brain can rewire itself to form new habits and behaviours.

> An analogy I personally love to use is of footpaths in the forest. As people use a path, it becomes clearer and more worn due to the usage. The vegetation underneath has little chance of regrowing due to the constant interruption of footsteps.
>
> However, if everyone started to use a different path, then the old path would start to grow over with vegetation, leaving the new path becoming more worn and defined. Soon the old path would cease to exist to the naked eye and would be of no use. This therefore provides some plausibility to the popular phrase, 'Use it before you lose it!'

Some of the latest research in neuroscience has suggested that not only can we create new brain cells through the process of neurogenesis, but that those new brain cells can assume the existing connections which are currently being used by old brain cells. The brand new 'worker' cells in the brain take over the role of the 'retiring' workers, whose impact starts to fade away. This gives an extra literal meaning to the words, 'Let it go'.

The creation of neural pathways (footpaths) in the brain occurs through thoughts, feelings and actions being repeated over time. Subsequently these neural pathways lead us to behaviours which become automated – otherwise commonly known as habits.

Exercise 1

As you have seen that the brain can change at any age, what three skills would you like to learn over the next ten years? e.g. scuba diving, speaking a new language or painting with watercolours.

Decide on one concrete thing you can do very soon to make it more likely that you will achieve those goals, e.g. spend 15 minutes a day on Duolingo to start learning Spanish.

Exercise 2

What fears, worries and doubts would you like to now start letting go of? Make a list.

I'd like you to ponder a question. Why is it that some people talk about learning techniques for help with personal issues, with great initial positive changes in their life, only to later complain about "slipping back" to old ways of thinking and feeling? People have reported feeling good for three to six months, then for some reason unknown to them, the happiness and well-being which they had initially experienced appears to fade. Subsequently, over time, they describe feeling no different to the time before they had initially received any help or experienced any change.

There are many theories as to why this happens, and in my experience of dealing with people who fall back in comparison to people who maintain continued progress, one word can be applied here: commitment. Unfortunately, when things are going right for an individual in their life after creating good habits, standards can potentially start to slip. I term this the period of 'success blindness'. Whereas the individual used to journal or exercise six days a week to maintain optimum well-being, they now do it only two to three times a week.

Within this book there are a plethora of tools and strategies which I sincerely hope you relentlessly adopt and keep up over the next 100 days. As has been stressed throughout this chapter, the process of repetition can produce changes in your brain at the cellular level. Your actions and responses to the outside world therefore can affect the interior world, but you need to keep up the new habits for this to happen.

As you should understand with complete certainty by now, letting go of old unproductive bad habits can completely transform your life.

Case study

Melanie

A client of mine recently mentioned that her greatest ambition was to let go of the bad habit of emotional eating at night, but that she did not know what to replace it with. She readily admitted that this had therefore created a fear of failure. This created a sense of frustration which resulted in her getting progressively more and more angry with herself.

Over a 37-day period (though please note that different people take different time periods to achieve things), she went on to install the habit of a nightly 15-minute session of yoga, reading a few pages of an autobiography and eating healthy, nutritious food. In this case, snacking involved slices of raw vegetables, e.g. carrots and cucumber. With time, she discovered that she felt more in control of her life, with her greatest reward being that she was far more in control of her emotions. She had successfully let go of frustration, anger, resentment and her fear of failure.

I often ask attendees at my workshops the following question: 'What is the quickest way to learn Italian?' Often they will suggest online courses, apps or evening classes. Occasionally someone will say, "Go to Italy and live there!" If you went to live in a village in the middle of nowhere in Italy and a relative came and visited you a year later, the probability is that you would be speaking Italian. The fastest method to learn anything, as you can see with how children learn, is to dive into the subject. By immersing yourself into the material of this book, you will absorb the contents with less distraction than if it was just a side hobby.

TIP: I highly recommend you practise the tools and strategies in this book for a minimum of 100 days, and follow the exercises suggested. Individually, the techniques and tools are effective. However, using them in conjunction with each other highly magnifies their effectivity. This is one of the reasons I know that this book can assist you long-term in letting go of behaviours, thoughts and/or feelings that currently plague you. Persist with the techniques, and you stand more chance of succeeding. Carry the book in your handbag or bag. It's all about your commitment to letting go, in order to change your life for the better.

10

The FIT Mind Model®

'You only live once. But if you work it right, once is enough.'
~ Fred Allen

Let me start with a question I have often asked audiences. "If you could let go of the bad past right now, how would you feel?" The responses I've received have all been of a similar type. People almost always respond with one of the following three words: "Free", "Happier", "Lighter".

I then usually follow up with another question: "If you could let go of your negative thoughts and worrying about the future, how would you feel?" Often the answers include: "Relieved", "Happy", "Hopeful" and "I will be able to sleep better!"

The mind has a tendency to wander. It can start focusing on the events of the past. Similarly, it can focus on future events which have not actually happened. In both cases, it often leads to us feeling unpleasant emotions.

Scenario 1

Imagine that you are driving a car on to a main street. You have your hands on the steering wheel as you press the accelerator down. Now imagine that you are only looking into your rear-view mirror instead of looking ahead. What could happen? Of course, you will eventually crash. By constantly looking behind us in life, we will miss out on what's happening now – what's in front of us.

Scenario 2

> Conversely, imagine walking down the street juggling several tennis balls, which represent your thoughts based in the future. This is the equivalent of overthinking or worrying. This takes most of your concentration and leaves you constantly distracted from what's happening around you right now. What do you think will eventually happen? You will drop the balls, as overwhelm takes over in the form of anxiety. You feel both drained and exhausted.

When I started working with people who were looking to improve an area of their life, I soon discovered that they all had one thing in common. They had difficulty in letting go of something. The things that they had to let go of were either rooted in the past or the future, but were impacting on the present moment. The objections to letting go included not wanting to give up on principles, fighting for a cause and being seen as weak or as condoning what had happened in the past.

What I went on to discover is that upon letting go of a negative belief such as 'I'm not worthy' or 'I'm not clever enough', their life started to change. People would change when they started to let go of a fear of meeting new people or a fear of the unknown. They would feel better when they let go of procrastinating or people-pleasing. Stress and anxiety levels started to reduce when they let go of needing to be perfect, obsessing about their wedding being 'the best wedding ever' or panicking about being caught up in traffic with no way to get to the business meeting in time.

The major discovery and realisation was that letting go was not just letting go of the past. It also involved letting go of the future. When referring to the future, it is to be emphasised that it includes the next minutes of your present day.

To demonstrate the timeline of an individual's life and where the act of letting go could assist them in reaching a

state of increased well-being, I created the FIT Mind Model®
for awareness purposes.

Having worked with people who are depressed, it is evident
that they often report that they 'can't see' a future, or that it
appears 'black and grey'. Hence their thoughts may primarily
be based in the past.

Many worriers and anxiety sufferers are often self-
confessed overthinkers, thinking about events and situations
which haven't yet happened. Their thoughts therefore appear
to be predominantly based in the future.

A third group of people with both depression and anxiety
experience thoughts which appear to fluctuate between the
past and the future.

I felt all three groups needed to let go of a behaviour, belief,
emotional need, opinion or fear which was keeping them
unhappy or unfulfilled in an area of their life.

I therefore created the FIT Mind Model® to demonstrate
where the mind can become focused, and how by letting go,
you can experience so much more in life. After all, we are
not born time travellers, flitting between the present and the
past and/or future. The only thing in your control is the very
moment you are occupying. However, much to our annoyance,
the mind can occupy various moments in time, which can
sometimes lead to emotional problems.

Have you ever suddenly found yourself in an unhappy
mood when the thought of a person from the past crossed your
mind? Have you ever found yourself anxious upon thinking
thoughts of worry and dread related to a meeting you were
going to attend later that week? So much so that you couldn't
sleep? Where we put our focus, our emotions can follow.

Letting go is a continual daily practice which requires
constant self-awareness, self-acceptance and self-regulation.
In this book, I will present the tools and techniques for this.
The FIT Mind Model® is an awareness tool. It is designed to
be a reminder that letting go is like brushing your teeth. It
has to be repeated daily to receive maximum benefits. Once it

becomes a habit and a practice, your self-awareness increases and you start feeling more in control of your life.

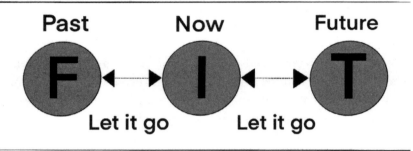

The FIT Mind Model® has three distinct sections. These sections denote the past, the present and the future. Our mind tends to focus daily on all three of these areas in time. The proportion of time spent in each region varies between individuals. Ideally, for optimum well-being, the mind would focus mostly on the 'now', leading to more 'in the moment' experiences.

As you observe the FIT Mind Model® from left to right, you immediately notice the letters F, I and T. F stands for Forgiveness (and the lack of it), the I stands for In the moment, and the T stands for Trust and Tenacity, which are needed to move forward past negative thinking.

As you see on the diagram, between each of the letters is a two-directional arrow denoting a fluid mind, which can move between F and I, or I and T. The optimum focus for the mind, as mentioned previously, is to remain at I (In the moment).

What the FIT Mind Model® proposes is that true letting go of the past involves forgiveness for events that happened in the past, and of the people in the event – including yourself.

Forgiveness here is not defined as acceptance or admission that what happened in the past was morally correct or OK. Instead it is a voluntary release of the negative feelings of resentment, bitterness, criticism, guilt and anger which may have accumulated over time.

The act of releasing these negative emotions is the 'letting go', which encourages the mind of the individual to move towards the 'In the moment' now.

Examples of thoughts focusing on past events include the following:

- "Why me?"
- "If only I had taken that job."
- "If only I had sat my exams."
- "If only I had accepted his marriage proposal – now he's marrying someone else."
- "If only I had gone to the funeral."
- "What if I had not driven so fast that evening?"
- "What if I had resisted his charms?"
- "What if I had only stuck at the business? I could be rich by now."
- "What if I had told her that I loved her?"
- "Why did that happen to me and no-one else?"
- "Why is it only me who is picked on to do presentations?"
- "Why is the world against me?"
- "Why do I continually have all the bad luck?"

Forgiveness may involve forgiving yourself, or forgiving someone else. What is important is that residual negative emotions are brought to the surface, acknowledged, accepted and voluntarily let go. By releasing these negative emotions, the mind has an increased chance of focusing on what is important in life right now, rather than continually focusing on what happened in the past.

It is a well-known fact that a lot of people have difficulty engaging in the process of forgiveness. It is often mistakenly seen as a sign of freeing the person who is to blame for the pain that has happened – and that person could even be yourself. Sometimes the past event is so traumatic that the pain of forgiveness seems to outweigh the benefits of letting go.

The FIT Mind Model® demonstrates that forgiveness allows a person who is willing to forgive to be free from the emotional struggle of the past. By untethering yourself from the negative emotions of the past, you allow yourself to move towards a place of happiness in the now again.

The past, as we know, cannot be changed. This can be an emotional block for some people, who will ruminate over 'what might have been'. Time, though, can be the great thought changer. Forgiveness does not happen instantaneously in most cases. It takes time, effort and persistent hard work to let go of those negative emotions towards the past. As you recognise the benefits to both yourself and those around you, there is greater chance of forgiveness.

While processing the act of forgiveness, it may be useful to think about what can be learnt from the past which will empower you positively to move forward. This can then change your focus and outlook on life.

Case study

Jo

A lady called Jo attended a workshop of mine several years ago. At first, she appeared rather negative to the notion of the possibility of life change that I had offered the group during the first session. Her harsh words during the first three workshop sessions did not endear her to anyone in the room. Clearly she was angry about something that had happened in her life. As with all the workshops I have delivered, people are encouraged to learn the tools and strategies presented. Reluctantly, Jo started to practise the tools I'm giving you in this book.

During Week 4 of the course, Jo asked to speak to me outside of the seminar room. Having seen her negativity during the first few weeks of the course, I must admit I did wonder what she was about to say! What surprised and amazed me was what she went on to reveal. Jo had been raped 15 years before and as a result had seen anger management therapists, counsellors, psychotherapists, CBT professionals and psychiatrists. To her mind, she said, nothing had worked. She sobbed as she recounted the history of the previous decade.

She had realised during the *Let It Go* course that she was attending that she had been focusing her mind on the past, regularly pouring hate and vitriol on all men. She had lost faith in the opposite sex, and had initially found it difficult that a man was delivering the course that she was attending. Her initial reaction was to want to leave the course after the first week. However her 'gut feeling' had convinced her to stay.

The 'Aha' moment that Jo had experienced which catalysed her need to let go of her negative emotions hinged on several new truths in her mind. The first was that she realised that she could not change the past. She also realised she no longer had to know 'why' she had been raped. That wasn't going to change anything. Finally she began to realise that by focusing on hating the man who had raped her, she had been giving him power over her self-esteem and self-worth. This she was no longer willing to do. She suddenly – for the first time in 15 years – felt like Jo the victor, and not Jo the victim.

The FIT Mind Model® proposes that the I represents being most present in 'In the moment' thinking. Imagine that you're at a family BBQ. The BBQ starts at 2 p.m., with everyone excited at this reunion. Delicious food is served, music plays and great conversation ensues. Then, in the blink of an eye, it's suddenly

10 o'clock at night! We often hear comments such as "Where has the time gone?" or "Wow, time seems to have disappeared and now it's dark!"

When we are focusing on the moment and are in state of joy, life seems to flow effortlessly and with ease. Thoughts about the future or the past have hardly impacted on our day, because we were focused mainly in the moment, and the joy that it brought.

Case study

Todd

I remember speaking to a client about his love of surfing. He would venture out to the local beach several times every week and engage in his passion. This would bring him so much joy and happiness, he said. I questioned him as to what it was about surfing that appealed to him. and made him so happy. He went on to tell me that it was that feeling of 'nothingness'. Whilst he was surfing, he would not 'think'. Thoughts about the past or future would disappear. He described how this brought him "into the moment" and how he had always felt this "ironic wave of calmness amongst the volatile nature of the waves" around him. The word that he kept repeating during our conversation was 'joy'.

For me personally, living in the moment does bring you feelings of joy, freedom, abundance, and gratitude for being alive.

The third segment of the FIT Mind Model®, T, is the Trust and Tenacity section.

Have you ever been in the shower and suddenly had a thought about someone? You then proceed to have an in-depth conversation with this person even though they are not there. Within minutes you are starting to feel emotions such as anger or anxiety, as you have started to believe elements of the conversation as truth.

You have essentially 'worked yourself up into a state'!

Even though the future has not happened, we are very fond of judging, making suppositions and assuming future events will play out exactly as we have visualised. Psychologists term this type of thinking 'catastrophe thinking'. It can be described as shuttling between irrational thoughts and worst-case-scenario thinking. As these thoughts build up in our mind, we start to develop negative emotions, leading us to a cycle of further negative thinking.

Thoughts which can dominate our cycle of focus can include:

- "What if I don't pass my exam?"
- "What if I don't lose the weight before the wedding?"
- "What if I can't afford the car payments?"
- "What if he spends the weekend with her while I'm away on my work trip?"
- "What's going to happen if it's all true, and she has been embezzling?"
- "What's going to happen if they can't find our hotel reservation?"
- "What's going to happen if I can't make the cake in time for his birthday?"
- "What's going to happen if I can't get to the meeting in time? Will I lose my job?"

Again, the above list is by no means exhaustive!

Letting go of the future involves embracing trust (T), as seen on the FIT Mind Model®. That is easier said than done, but when the emotion of trust exceeds the emotion of uncertainty, we are able to return to the present moment, leaving us feeling more hopeful and secure.

Again, we're back to the message of this book: *Let It Go*.

Overthinking and worry, which produce feelings of anxiety, can be short-circuited partly by adopting a more trusting approach. This, combined with taking daily actions towards your goals, can reduce your worry, anxiety and daily stresses.

If you were to re-examine what has happened in your life and to record all the moments where you had worried about future events, only to experience a more positive result than you expected, you would see that most of the time we worry over nothing.

Perhaps a better way of viewing this would be through this simple question: Throughout your life, what percentage of your worries have ever come true?

Letting go of a future event that is consuming you with worry and stress, and trusting that life can work in your favour, brings you back into the moment. After all, what benefits has worrying ever really given you?

 TIP: It's worth taking a photo of the FIT Mind Model® diagram and discussing it with a friend.

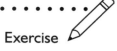

Exercise

Print out or photocopy the FIT Mind Model® diagram and place it somewhere where you can see it regularly. This can act as a powerful reminder to practise the tools in this book, and to actively seek to focus on the now.

11

Introducing the Power Statements

'Arguing with a fool proves there are two.'
~ Doris M Smith

Integral to the *Let It Go* process is series of affirmations and questions – the Power Statements. They will become instinctive thoughts over time, automatic triggers to shepherd your thinking back on track whenever it veers off course.

There's nothing mystical about committing to these. They become ingrained through repetition. It's important to stick them up around your house to remind yourself of them, and to recite them until they become second nature. It might feel artificial at first, but if you make this practice part of your daily routine, they can really transform your thinking.

Remember that you first start the thinking process when you wake. Often though, with many people, this first thinking of the day is worry, negativity and fear. Therefore I highly recommend you write the Power Statements on post-it notes and stick them up near to where you wake up in the morning. They should be placed strategically where you can see them with ease. The effectivity of the Power Statements will diminish if you place them in a book with the intention of reading them first thing. You will eventually put the book back on the shelf and forget the contents.

Place the post-it notes:
- by your bed
- in your bathroom
- on a mirror
- on your fridge
- by the front door of your home

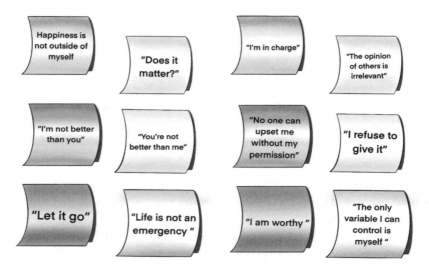

The Power Statements were not meant to be designed like simple affirmations, such as 'I am happy', 'I am rich', 'I am healthy' or 'I am a millionaire'. They are designed to act like a grenade being thrown into your subconscious mind, in order to disrupt your current unhelpful thought patterns.

A vast amount of research has indicated the positive effect of repeating daily statements and affirmations. In the *Journal of American College Health*, a study found that using affirmations decreased symptoms of depression and negative thinking, and increased levels of self-esteem. I would recommend you using the Power Statements offered in this chapter in conjunction with the other tools and strategies in this book. I would also highly recommend that you reread the book six months after this first read, as ideas often take time to embed and take effect.

I'd suggest writing a note in your diary now as a reminder for this. Now let's move on to the first Power Statement.

I. LET IT GO!

This Power Statement is the mother of them all, and the absolute key to the process.

Case study

> ### Rob
>
> A man attended my course. Although I didn't recognise it initially, his prevailing mood was anger. At the end of the six-week 'Let It Go' programme, he and his wife approached me and told me that his wife had booked them a holiday abroad.
>
> "Great!" I said, and he responded, "No, you don't understand. My wife hasn't wanted to go on holiday for about ten years!"
>
> When I asked him why he replied, "Because I would always start an argument at the bar or the pool. I was Mr Angry and I would argue with everyone."
>
> He had suffered anger-management issues for many years. He had seen psychologists, counsellors and even a psychiatrist, but nothing had worked.
>
> He went on to explain that before the course, if I had cut him up on the road, he would have been very confrontational – to the point where he might even have followed me home to confront me.
>
> He said that the Power Statement 'Let It Go' had been fundamental in his transformation. He no longer loses his temper quickly because through repetition of this statement, it has embedded itself into his subconscious and therefore into his Blueprint.
>
> He started laughing and said that his friends and family now try to 'push his buttons' to get a reaction out of him, but he has

chilled out so much that it just doesn't work. So at the end of the course, he had changed to such an extent that his wife felt comfortable booking a holiday, knowing that she would relax and enjoy it rather than being anxious as to when he would lose his temper.

I recently heard they have been away on holiday 11 times since he attended the course, which is amazing evidence that this process can help all sorts of people with all sorts of different problems. Now when someone cuts him up, he focuses on the Power Statement 'Let It Go'.

He's calmer and more in control as a result. He knows that it is likely that he will catch up to the person who cut him up at the next traffic light and therefore that he hasn't lost any time. He reasons that the person who cut him up is more likely to be stopped by the police for speeding. In the long run, it hasn't changed anything in his life directly. They aren't being disrespectful to him personally – it is just the way they are.

2. LIFE IS NOT AN EMERGENCY

Make a mental note to take stock of the atmosphere you sense amongst the people around you for the next week or so. Whether you're in the office, on your commute or at the school gates, observe how people rush about. They will be talking on their phones, walking hastily past you, looking preoccupied. They are racing to meet a deadline, late for a meeting, stressed, distracted, multitasking. We've all become so impatient. Technology has created a culture of instant gratification, and we feel disappointed whenever people (including ourselves) don't behave with the efficiency of devices. We get frustrated at any sign of time-wasting: a relative who takes six rambling sentences to convey information that could fit into one; an overcrowded London Underground platform that means we have to wait an extra ten minutes to catch a train; a longer than average queue in the coffee shop.

When you are around people who are in a hurry, rushing and frantically moving, what type of energy can you feel? Does it feel positive or negative? Even the feeling of being in a hurry evokes feelings of negative frenetic energy.

The simple act of deciding not to stress over these totally insignificant inconveniences is surprisingly liberating. It's a way to reclaim a whole load of wasted energy, because that restless, frustrated feeling is totally pointless. It doesn't make you any more efficient, or focused. You get no more done and your state of mind is only made more jittery and agitated as a result of it.

Let go of it and you'll feel calmer and less anxious. This will change your thinking, a sign that your Blueprint is beginning to change at a deep level.

3. DOES IT MATTER?

Sometimes we can make things matter which we shouldn't even give a second thought. For example, we can't stop thinking about an exchange of words with a customer on the phone earlier. This lowers our mood, and then goes on to affect the rest of our working day. Think of the things in your life that you have held onto emotionally, and it has affected your mood. You may have attended a social gathering after an altercation with your partner, and let the feeling fester in your mind. As you approached the gathering, you could not stop having verbal digs at your partner. This then resulted in a night of tension between you both. When you feel yourself getting agitated, it may be wise to stop for a moment and ask yourself, "Does it matter?" It's a quick way to regain your sense of humour and perspective.

You may be in a supermarket looking for a vital ingredient for the Greek dish that you are planning to prepare that evening. Much to your annoyance, you find it is not on the shelves. They have sold out. You had set your heart on cooking this dish for your new boyfriend, and now feel that your evening is in ruins. You had really wanted to impress him. Sometimes we place such high expectations or importance on something having to go our way that when it fails to do so, our world appears to fall apart. Where in your life could the words 'Does it matter?' apply right now? What unnecessary high expectations could you let go of?

When things have not gone my way, or the day has felt like a total disaster, I will say to myself, 'Tomorrow I can always make a comeback!'

Ten seconds later

Does it matter?

No!

4. HAPPINESS IS NOT OUTSIDE OF MYSELF

Regarding this Power Statement, if 'happiness is not outside of myself', then where is it?

We all have an intrinsic understanding of this. Even so, it is one of the hardest statements to grasp. It's human nature to seek satisfaction in external situations: relationships, experiences (such as holidays), material things – from the homes we live in to the clothes we wear. Even when we know that the things on our wish list will offer only fleeting happiness or distraction, their hold over us is still powerful and the associated wish-granting myth, the idea that when x happens, or when you change y, you'll finally 'be happy', retains an enormous power over us.

Common examples of this type of thinking include:

I will be happy when...
...I lose weight
...I get a new kitchen
...I find a new man
...I book a holiday
...I buy a new car
...I get that dress for the wedding
...I get a six pack for the summer
...the client signs the contract
...the weather improves

The common denominator is 'I will be happy when...' This is therefore attaching conditions which are future-based to your happiness.

So how should you combat this by persuading your brain to recognise that happiness is within? Mantras such as 'I'm happy' or 'I feel happy' just don't work. Your brain's bullshit detector goes off immediately. In contrast, the statement 'Happiness is not outside of myself' is less of an affirmation and more of a fact. Even if you don't feel happy as you recite it, it's inherently true. You can't force your mind to accept something you don't

125

believe, but you can shift your focus by resetting false beliefs and replacing them with true ones.

If happiness is not outside of yourself, it is within you. We've all repeated variations of the 'I'll be happy when...' statements above to ourselves. The list is endless. But all of the evidence shows that outside influences and material things have only a minor impact on overall happiness levels. What's more, this effect is only temporary.

The problem with thinking this way is that in doing so, you are giving your power away. You are putting your happiness outside of yourself. You're sending a message to your Blueprint that you will be happy if something (outside of yourself) happens. Your Blueprint absorbs this information and renounces responsibility for your happiness, and you find yourself stuck in a state of perpetual dissatisfaction.

I love this from the Dr Seuss children's book *Oh! The Places You'll Go!* Essentially, when you decide happiness is outside of yourself, you're stuck in the waiting place...

Waiting for the fish to bite
or waiting for the wind to fly a kite
or waiting around for Friday night
or waiting, perhaps, for their Uncle Jake
or a pot to boil, or a Better Break
or a string of pearls, or a pair of pants
or a wig with curls, or Another Chance.
Everyone is just waiting.

Ask yourself, honestly, whether you're pinning your happiness on something far off. If so, resolve now to reclaim control over it.

5. I'M NOT BETTER THAN YOU, YOU'RE NOT BETTER THAN ME

Case study

Lynsey

An attendee of a *Let It Go* programme was often bullied by one particular manager in the office. One day in the corridor, the manager again spoke down to Lynsey, and barked criticism regarding Lynsey's latest project results. This time the Power Statement 'I'm not better than you, you're not better than me' flashed before Lynsey's eyes. As a result of the shift in confidence she had experienced by internalising this statement, she no longer felt she had to listen to the manager's negative comments. Immediately she raised her hand and placed it palm outwards in front of the offending manager's face. Lynsey then informed the manager never to speak to her like that again, otherwise she would report her. The manager, who was shocked to see Lynsey's strong stance, turned away hurriedly. The manager later apologised in private. She now treats Lynsey with more respect. If you don't value yourself, then others may not value or respect you either.

This Power Statement implies that all people are of the same value. With time and after repetition, it can become a strong belief. You should have no problem talking to someone who is, for example, a millionaire or a lot more senior than you in your company. Even millionaires and people in high-powered jobs have their own personal struggles and anxieties. We are all human and have emotional baggage that is weighing us down. Just because someone else may be wealthier or more successful than you at this moment in time, it doesn't mean they are necessarily happy, nor does it mean they are better than you. They have just found a way of having status in the world's eyes. That does not equate to worth in real terms.

As a good friend of mine says, 'Everyone shits, showers and shaves,' regardless of what background they stem from. Conversely, the statement also applies to us. We are also no better than anyone else.

Case study

Gary

I'll always remember a client who was a lawyer. He mentioned that this was one of his favourite Power Statements. He used it to transform his attitude when he attended a job interview for a highly esteemed position in a law firm. Previously he had been overlooked after interviews for similar positions. He had attributed this to his own lack of confidence. At past interviews, he had always felt a sense of inferiority in front of the interviewers, which he knew originated from his working-class roots. He had come from poor beginnings and had found it difficult to shift the feeling of being an 'outsider to the establishment'.

At this latest interview he knew in his mind that he was the equal of anyone in the room.

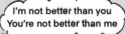

I'm not better than you
You're not better than me

This translated into his new confident attitude. He was offered the job the very next day.

6. THE OPINIONS OF OTHERS ARE IRRELEVANT. IT'S WHAT I THINK ABOUT MYSELF THAT MATTERS.

Scenario 1

Imagine that a lady has gone to a wedding do. Throughout the night she is complimented on the way she looks. Naturally, she is happy as she continues to enjoy the evening. By the end of the night she has received 99 compliments. As she is leaving the wedding with her husband, she hears a rude comment regarding a black dress directed towards where she is standing. She has no clear idea who has thrown the insult, nor about whom. There are a number of other women around her, some with black dresses. However, she is convinced that the insult was addressed to her, even though there is no logic to this. On the way home in the car, what do you think she is focused on: the 99 compliments or the 1 insult? All the compliments have now been washed away and have been replaced by the one negative comment.

No matter what others think and say, it's what we truly believe which becomes our truth. No matter how many people tell us we are good enough, if we don't feel this, then that becomes our reality. An example could be someone wanting to start a new business, but continually putting it off. They fear not succeeding, even though family tell them to go and follow their dreams.

People laughed at Arnold Schwarzenegger when he declared that he would like to be a Hollywood actor. They scoffed that he couldn't speak English, let alone act! Schwarzenegger did not agree. He worked out for six hours a day, and took night classes in acting as well as learning to speak English. The only opinion that Schwarzenegger believed was his own.

7. THE ONLY VARIABLE I CAN CONTROL IS MYSELF

This simply reflects the fact that you can't control others. You can't control their thoughts or their actions. However, changing the way you behave, think and react can lead to powerful shifts in the way that other people feel around you, and as a result, can have a transformative effect even on bad relationships and negative situations that seem insurmountable.

Many of us know someone who is said to be 'controlling'. This person tries to control the behaviour of other individuals by conditioning them.

This is doomed to fail, as it is impossible to control someone else's thinking. There is no way of controlling the outcome or guaranteeing a reaction from another person, although those who are skilled manipulators may come close.

Whenever you feel the need to try to control another person, it's important to remember that it's a sign that you're feeling out of control yourself due to an existing insecurity. Controlling people need to control others in order to feel they have a sense of self-mastery. Some event may have happened to them in the past which has left them feeling not in control. Now this need to feel in control is part of their everyday behaviour. If they don't feel in control, they may feel anxiety. I personally know people who become anxious if they don't have the television remote control near them!

The only variable I can control is myself

Even with our own children, we can attempt to guide them, but we can't control them. The only healthy focus to cultivate is the ability to control ourselves.

8. THE PAST DOES NOT DEFINE ME

If you were to try to navigate your way out of a car park using only your rear-view mirror, it would be just a matter of time before you crashed. So why look to the past when you should be focusing on the road in front of you? It's time to move forward, let go of the past ('Let It Go') and set your eyes straight ahead. Your past does not define you. Whatever has happened, good or bad, has gone now. In order to move forward, it is better to think forward.

By continually focusing on the past and revisiting events and situations, you run the risk of missing out on your present life. Do you know anyone who continually talks about past events? Where is their mind focused and how does it impact on their life?

Unfortunately, some people do have a fear of the past repeating itself. They fear that the past does equal the future. Hence they find it difficult to form a new romantic relationship, or trust any new people they meet. They can be suspicious and start comparing people against an internal checklist they possess. This mistrust of people can transfer its way into the workplace, and possibly make them difficult people to communicate with.

Exercise

Here is a question I would like you to ponder on:

If you couldn't remember any of your baggage from the past, or you could remember it but it didn't affect you any more emotionally, how do you think you would feel?

The top three most common answers that I have heard are: 'Free', 'Lighter' and 'Happier'.

9. NO-ONE CAN UPSET ME WITHOUT MY PERMISSION. I REFUSE TO GIVE IT

You have much more control than you think. When we get upset, it is actually our own choice to get upset. The choice happens in milliseconds and is based on our mindset at the Blueprint level. Have you noticed that certain people can upset you more than others? Often our parents can upset us more than our boss or partner at home.

We can, though, consciously take back control of our emotions. This starts with our own thoughts.

Increased mental strength comes from choice. When we consciously realise that we do have a choice, then our mental resilience to external events can increase dramatically. I'm not saying that you will never get upset again, but this Power Statement will give you the opportunity to develop some mental muscle.

'No one can upset me without my permission. I refuse to give it' states that in order for someone to emotionally get under your skin, you need to allow them to. No one has a gun to your head. No one is telling you to get

132

upset or forcing you to cry. It's your choice. You are in charge of the way you react. It's down to the ultimate ownership of your feelings.

Once you realise that, it's a powerful game-changer. You can't point at someone and blame them for making you upset, as you are the one allowing yourself to get upset.

Try this neat little trick: make a pointing action with one of your hands. What do you notice about your fingers? Your index finger, and perhaps your thumb, is pointing in front of you, but where are the other fingers? They're pointing right back at you.

By blaming someone else for the way that you're feeling, you are pointing once at them and three times back towards yourself. You are allowing them to upset you with your permission. You are giving away your power and control.

Every time you blame, complain, judge, expect, criticise or assume, you are giving away your personal power.

'No one can upset me without my permission. I refuse to give it' assists you in reclaiming your internal power.

10. GUARD YOUR MIND

Our mind is subject to the daily noise of the world at large. We are bombarded with information from external sources such as news media, entertainment, social media, family, friends, work colleagues and neighbours. All this information can influence us, to a level where we feel overwhelmed. This can push us into anxiety, fear and worry. Because more information is readily available than ever before, sometimes it is good to become aware that our mind is under constant attack from the outside world and step back. What we expose our mind to does affect how we feel, so perhaps it's a good idea to remind ourself of this.

Seeing the 'Guard Your Mind' post-it note will be a reminder of the negative influences that exist in this world and which can potentially affect you. It also serves to encourage you to maintain the daily self-awareness that you can practise as you move forward.

We go to the doctor/dentist for check-ups in order to avoid any potential health problems. Who do we go to to see about our mind? Unless you have the budget for regular therapy, you have to take care of this yourself. It is also a known problem that many men won't seek help in this area, as it can be seen as emasculating, embarrassing or weak.

Your mind requires daily maintenance in the same way your body does in order to function correctly. Imagine a daily ritual to aid you in keeping your mind healthy, vibrant, relaxed and focused. There is a suite of practices which you can select from which may assist you in reflecting, refocusing and revitalising your mindset. These include meditation, journaling, exercise, massage and gratitude. Throughout this book you will find a number of exercises, tools and strategies to help you maintain this healthy mindset.

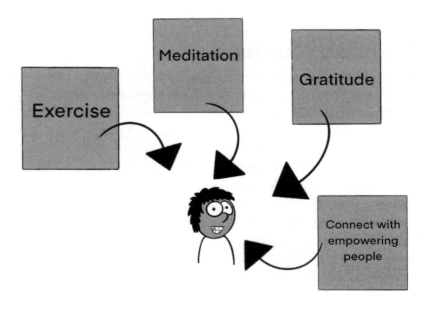

II. WHERE FOCUS GOES, ENERGY FLOWS

The brain has a special area dedicated to focusing on what you are currently thinking about. It's called the reticular activating system (RAS). Have you ever bought a new car and then the same day you see exactly the same model on the corner of a street? It then starts to appear everywhere, like magic! The truth is, it was everywhere already. You were just not interested and therefore didn't register it. When we start to focus on something in particular, our brain acts in conjunction with our new-found focus, to bring it into our 'line of sight'. Suddenly we see our car everywhere. It could be that you're on holiday in Florida. You are sitting in a restaurant having lunch. As you enjoy your food, someone sitting at a table near you mentions your favourite football team. Instantly you home in on what this person has just said. Our brain has an inordinate capacity to focus in on what it thinks we want or are interested in. As Tony Robbins says, 'Where focus goes, energy flows.' If you can apply the logic from this, then it goes without saying that if you're focused on what's negative about life, you will 'see' more of it, and vice versa.

This important brain function of filtering out information and only focusing on specific details is designed to stop us from suffering overwhelm. Otherwise we would be driven insane. Out of the estimated 11 million bits of information we receive through our senses per second, we can focus on fewer than 50. This filter system then allows us to focus on what we perceive to be important at that moment.

Case study

Andy

A client was overly focused on not losing money in his business. Hence his mind was focused on saving money, rather than making money. In essence, he discovered that he had a fear of loss. This

135

stemmed from his childhood, seeing his single mother struggle with money. She would constantly bellow well-known phrases such as 'Money doesn't grow on trees'. This would bring him anxiety, worry and sleepless nights. When he retrained his mind to let go of the fear of loss, let go of the negative beliefs that he had learnt from his mother, and focus on making money through better customer service and innovation, his business started to grow. Every time this feeling of fear of loss subsequently appeared, he would immediately focus on the words 'Let It Go' and 'Where Focus Goes, Energy Flows'. He would then remind himself to focus on success in his business, not on losing money.

Scenario 2

Imagine that a woman is excited about a special holiday to Bali that her family has planned. When she starts trying on new swimwear, she feels disheartened and frustrated. She has gained 15 lbs in weight. She starts to have a conversation with herself about needing to have that beach body within the next four months. Her brain immediately focuses on ways to lose weight. She thinks about the diets she has been on previously. This time, however, she wants to try something different. Suddenly, as if by magic, everywhere she seems to look there are magazines, TV weight-loss shows and online programmes on how to shed those undesirable pounds. Her relentless focus takes her on a successful journey which sees her reaching her target weight loss.

Scenario 3

A guy is sitting all alone in his apartment on a dark winter's night. The apartment is cold, as he opens his post. He starts to feel anxious as all he can see are bills. He worries about his lack of money, and starts to question why he is bothering working at all. His relationship with his girlfriend has just ended, and life appears to be one problem after another. As he sits there, he thinks 'In life, it never rains, it just pours.'

Suddenly, out of the corner of his eye, he sees blue flashing lights outside. He notices two of the houses opposite his apartment are on fire. Within seconds he runs outside to see if he can assist in any way. There are fire engines, police and ambulances. People are screaming and crying in the street. For the next two hours he helps by offering hot drinks, blankets and biscuits. After the blaze has been extinguished, it is clear that the houses have been severely damaged. However, more importantly, everyone is safe.

How do you think he could be feeling? Good, because he has helped people? Grateful that he has a home? Where has his previous anxiety gone? During his time helping out, he shifted his mental focus. As a consequence his anxiety, worries and low mood lifted. His sense of self-worth has increased.

Shifting our focus involves taking action. The action that we have to take can often be at odds with how we are feeling. Remember: feelings will always arise – they cannot be stopped. We do have a choice on how to think and act, though. This is the power that we have within us. Choice.

12. I AM ENOUGH

The feeling of not being good enough or worthy enough are commonplace everywhere. Wherever I have worked, I have met people who openly say things like, 'I don't feel good enough.' It's a symptom of society, with social media encouraging comparisons which lead to conditions such as 'Facebook

137

depression' being talked about. Overuse of social media sites such as Instagram and Snapchat have been seen by researchers to be linked with increased loneliness and depression.

A lack of self-worth develops over a period of time. Events and experiences shape our version of our reality and instil a perception of who we think we are and where we think we fit into this world. As a result of constantly comparing ourself with others, we formulate an opinion and belief about ourselves. This forms the basis of our self-worth. A lack of self-worth can hinder progress in any area of your life you'd care to mention.

For several decades I suffered a lack of self-worth because of my 'story'. It is my personal mission to elevate others who lack self-worth, and to help them understand that no-one is better than them, and vice versa. It's how we think which differentiates us from each other.

The Power Statement 'I am enough' is an extremely powerful and valuable tool to use to elicit a change from within. These words are the antithesis of negative and low self-worth, and over time can help defuse the negative self-image that resides within so many people. When you actually say the words 'I am enough', a voice from inside might debate their validity. This internal saboteur may try to block your acceptance of the words. Keep saying these words at random times such as when you are making dinner, mowing the lawn or driving the car. Please expect resistance from within. No-one ever said change was easy.

A bamboo seed can take up to seven years to break through the surface of the soil. In that time it still has to be fed and watered. Eventually it will break through the surface, and can within one week grow a spectacular 14 feet.

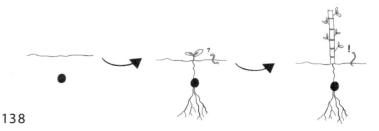

13. YOU CAN'T CHANGE WHAT YOU CAN'T CONTROL, AND YOU CAN'T CONTROL WHAT YOU CAN'T CHANGE.

Inevitably, most people worry at some point in their lifetime. This worry can lead to anxiety. If you were to examine the mind and where it is focused, you would realise that these thoughts are future based. This was discussed in the previous chapter, which introduced the FIT Mind Model®. When we feel not in control, we can feel vulnerable, exposed, trapped, uncertain and fearful. These feelings can consume us as we seek to gain or regain control.

Let me illustrate this with two examples:

1. A man is on his way to a job interview. As a rule, he always arrives at any meeting early, to prepare mentally and to relax. However, this time he is caught in a terrible traffic jam. He tries to call the office to inform them of his predicament, but cannot get a phone signal. His response is to start thinking anxious thoughts in his head. He feels frustrated and angry at the traffic situation. Thoughts such as 'I'm going to lose this dream job' and 'Just my luck!' start to play out in his mind.

2. You have made an offer on a piece of land and are awaiting a response from the seller. You know that you have a deadline to meet to acquire land for your building project. Three days have elapsed and you still haven't heard from the seller. This starts to play on your mind. Your gut feeling says that there is no problem, but your mind starts to race to possible worst-case scenarios. Your hands feel tied as you await the outcome.

14. I'M IN CHARGE

Have you ever felt powerless, not in control of your thoughts and emotions? So much so that you froze with fear? At that moment you felt helpless, and the negative thoughts can then spiral. This Power Statement is a reminder to yourself that you are in charge of your life. You could be on a running machine and your goal is to run for 45 minutes. At around the 30-minute mark, your mind starts to think thoughts of 'Maybe I've done enough and I should stop now.' The mind is set up to keep us safe – it is one of its primary functions. American ultra-marathon runner and retired Navy Seal David Goggins, in his book *Can't Hurt Me Now*, says he believes that most of us are capable of achieving 40% more in training, but that our mind tends to give up before we reach our full potential, and then we give up on our goal.

There will be moments when we doubt ourselves. For some people this is an ongoing emotional battle. The idea of regaining control of one's own destiny appears like a far-fetched fantasy.

Look at 'I'm in charge!' as a war cry. A declaration that you are in charge of your life. A declaration that you have decided to take full responsibility for your actions and behaviours, and that whatever has happened in the past has gone. Whatever happens in the future has not happened. What you do have is a choice – a choice to decide what you do next.

What if you could be doing more than you are currently doing in your life? What if you took charge of your life, rather than just let yourself be influenced by outside factors like other people, the media and social media? What if you decided to go and pursue that dream that you have been putting off? That journey that you would have made ages ago if you hadn't listened to your naysayers and subsequently taken no action.

Often we are afraid to take charge of our life because of the failures of our past. Remember, failure is just what hasn't worked. It doesn't define you. It's only a result of something that didn't work out. As life is temporary, so is failure. By deciding to take charge of your thinking, rather than letting your faulty thinking take charge of you, suddenly you become driven by your intent.

Have you ever reached an impasse where you decided 'Enough is enough!', and took action? Let the words of 'I'm in charge' inspire you take charge and drive you forward. It can be as simple as going for a promotion, instead of letting your fears of failing put you off. Remember that the fears you feel are physiological body reactions. You can't stop feelings showing up. However you <u>can</u> change how you respond. This starts with the decision to take charge.

In concluding this chapter, I highly recommend that you stick up the post-it notes showing the Power Statements in prominent places at home. Also perhaps place your favourite Power Statement in your wallet or purse. The more that you can immerse yourself, the faster the information will sink into your unconscious mind. It is from here that the Power Statements will actively influence you at various moments. Each of the Power Statements advocates and enriches a new way of thinking, helping you to let go of the outdated and unproductive thoughts which have held you back for so long.

TIP: Place the Power Statements around the house, and be sure to change them around after a month, or they can become 'white noise', and less effective. A highly effective place is the bathroom mirror. When you are brushing your teeth in the morning, you will see them. Place your favourite two or three Power Statements on or around the mirror.

Keep them displayed at home for at least 100 days (about three months) so they have time to become part of your Blueprint. If you are prepared to invest some time into this, you can go on and reap the rewards of positive change.

12

How Grateful Are You?

'This is a wonderful day. I've never seen it before.'
~ Maya Angelou

The Power Statements, practised regularly, help your brain to forge new pathways, ensuring that you reprogram your internal mindset. This habituates new thinking that is more helpful and empowering than the old, ingrained dysfunctional thoughts that have governed your perspective and influenced your behaviour until now.

But the Power Statements on their own are not enough to ensure the seismic shift required at a deep level. There are many other practices that will help to facilitate a lasting change in your Blueprint. One of these, which is absolutely key to letting go, is to cultivate an ATTITUDE OF GRATITUDE.

There's far more to this than trite *#blessed* posts on social media. Even if it feels false at first, building giving thanks into your daily habits eventually ensures that gratitude becomes a psychological reflex. It really is a wonderful thing. The more you notice the good stuff, the more you notice the good stuff. Simple.

In the words of Plato, 'A grateful mind is a great mind which eventually attracts to itself great things.'

There's an impressive wealth of scientific evidence to back up the fact that gratitude practices, from journaling to simply noting what goes right with your day, significantly influence overall happiness and life satisfaction.

There's nothing fluffy about the research on this. A study by psychologists at the University of California compared two groups of depressives. For ten weeks, the first group was challenged to write a gratitude diary, and the second group was asked to keep a diary of daily irritations. Those who kept the gratitude diary not only reported a more optimistic attitude at the end of the study, they had also exercised more and had made fewer visits to the doctor. Another US study pitted two groups of 20 clinically depressed volunteers against one another. The first group was taught a gratitude practice and asked to follow it, while the second group was told they would earn some money at the end of the trial but should continue their daily lives as normal. At the end of the study, the gratitude group reported significant improvements in their overall feelings about their life. Many felt happier than they had done in years.

The shift here has nothing to do with circumstances: it's all about perception. Gratitude practice teaches you to reframe life in a positive way, noticing and noting the positive things that happen, rather than skipping over them to focus on problems. Gratitude works the other way, too. Managers who express gratitude to their staff motivate them to work harder in future, as we all like to be acknowledged. It stands to reason.

And although what we're aiming for – in order to bring about a shift in your Blueprint – is a high frequency of grateful thoughts, even one-off gestures of gratitude can have enormously transformative power. Martin Seligman of the University of Pennsylvania, the renowned US 'father of Positive Psychology', encouraged subjects to write a letter to acknowledge the impact of a kindness the recipient had shown them. This task had greater and more lasting benefits than any other intervention in the study. The impact of this single act of active gratitude lasted for a month, on average. A whole month. That's remarkable.

In short, when it comes to the research on gratitude, there appears to be an endless upside. A psychologist from the University of Birmingham noted in 2013 that the "list of potential benefits of gratitude is almost endless... raised self-confidence, better work attitude, strengthened resiliency, less physical pain, improved health and longevity."

Some of the happiest people in the world live in remote places where they don't have much, but they are grateful for what they do have. They enjoy simple pleasures such as music, reading, family and nature. Material things can make you happy for a short period of time, but this doesn't last. You might buy a new outfit and find it makes you feel happy in the short term, but does that outfit still make you as happy two years later? Typically, no.

> I went to Cuba on holiday and whilst talking to a taxi driver, I mentioned that everyone seemed happier there. Everywhere I went, people were smiling and enjoying life. I couldn't understand why they were like that when, looking at their surroundings, they seemed poor. I asked the taxi driver why everyone was so happy and he replied, "Well, we have rum, cigars, music and beautiful landscapes. What more could you want out of life?" He went on to say that as a nation they don't have much, yet they feel they have everything. Perhaps it could be suggested that this is the opposite of many countries.

I was inspired by this incident and to this day his words have impacted on me, because he's right. It's the little things in life that make us happy. Gratitude for the little things is what fosters true happiness.

I'd like to encourage you to make a ritual of grateful thinking. Turn it into something you do often, throughout the day. The more you do it, the better you'll get at it. You'll soon be able to reel off a list of things you feel grateful for at the drop of a hat.

Scenario

I'd like to take you on a mental journey which I hope might help demonstrate how a shift in thinking can dramatically enhance your perspective on life, enabling you to feel hugely grateful for something you have taken entirely for granted until now.

Imagine you wake up tomorrow morning and everything appears oddly dark. You can't see anything in your room. You make your way to the light switch. Still no light. You then have to feel your way to the window, but can't see out of it. You can't see your hands in front of you. You have lost your sight.

As the reality of losing your sight hits you, how do you think you would be feeling? Frightened? Panicky?

So, within an hour, you are at the hospital and the doctors are running tests on your eyes. They get the results back and inform you that there is nothing physically wrong with your eyes, so they refer you to the neurology department to run further tests as to why you are unable to see. They carry out tests on your brain and find out that for some reason there's a lack activity in the part of the brain that is associated with your eyes. It simply isn't working. You are told that your eyes are actually fine, but it appears your brain is unable to process any information it's receiving, resulting in you having no sight.

The doctor then tells you that she doesn't understand why it's happened, but that your sight could come back in time. This gives you some of hope. You make an appointment to return in a few days for a check-up and you're told that, hopefully, your sight may have returned by then.

For the next few days, you are with family and friends and your eyesight hasn't yet returned. You go back to the hospital for the follow-up appointment and again they run tests on your eyes and your brain, but still there is no electrical activity in the part of your brain that processes vision. The consultant explains that sometimes this can happen without reason and there is nothing that can be done, medically, to restore your sight. She breaks the news to you that you will need to register as being visually impaired.

It suddenly dawns on you that might never see the faces of your loved ones again. Your driving licence will be taken away from you. Your independence will be restricted. Life is never going to be the same again.

How do you feel? Devastated? Angry? Frustrated? Depressed?

A week later, you receive assistance from the Royal National Institute for the Blind, who help you to adapt your home for your disability.

You're still devastated, feeling lost and fearful and lacking any hope that your sight will ever return. The practical adjustments to your life make the disability feel real.

You cry every time you dwell on it. You will probably never see sunshine or the sea again. You won't see your children's faces change and develop, as the remaining softness of childhood disappears and a grown-up face, with its distinctive characteristics, emerges. You won't watch the evening sky turn from golden to luminous red, or study a leaf up close. You will no longer be able to feast your eyes on a plate of longed-for food, or your beloved partner's face.

Would the problems you had before you lost your sight seem insignificant now? Some of them would. You would view life differently. What seemed vitally important before may no longer seem anywhere near as important now. You would probably give anything to have those problems back if it meant you had your sight back too.

Your outlook on life would be totally transformed.

As the months roll by and Christmas approaches, you realise that you will never see a Christmas tree again. You will never see the decorative lights in the street again.

The winter nights draw in and the clocks go back. It gets darker earlier, but it doesn't matter to you, because in your world, there's no difference between day and night. It doesn't matter what time of the year it is, or what time of the day it is.

One day in December, you wake up as normal, still feeling low, and make your way to the bathroom to brush your teeth. You have become good at feeling your way around your home and go to the bathroom sink, pick up your toothbrush and start brushing your teeth as usual. You can taste the mint flavour in your mouth. You never paid attention to things like this before, probably because you were too busy, but with your eyesight gone, your other senses are heightened.

You cry a lot still, and this morning you feel the tears running down your cheeks and the salty taste as they run past your lips.

You finish brushing your teeth and spit out the toothpaste into the sink, and watch the toothpaste running down the sink hole. You are shocked, and turn to see yourself in the mirror, your cheeks still wet with tears.

Within the hour you are at the hospital and they again run tests on your eyes and your brain. They don't know whether it was a blockage or a lesion, and can't explain why your eyesight has returned. But you have it back.

How do you feel now?

On top of the world?

So why aren't you grateful for your sight today?

Could this be a reminder to start focusing on what you actually have in life?

It's almost guaranteed that if you were suddenly sent to prison for three months, all your other problems would pale into total insignificance. When you were released from serving your time, you'd feel grateful for your freedom. You would want to kiss the pavement and enjoy the sunshine, and it would feel joyful simply to walk down the street at your leisure. It's easy to feel grateful for something you've lost then recovered, but if it's always there, it gets taken for granted. But partly, this is

a choice. Why not choose instead to be grateful for all these basic pleasures now?

By resolving to feel grateful for the fundamentals of your life, you gain a new, keen sense of good fortune. This feeling of abundance then helps to generate positive energy that ensures your good fortune perpetuates more of the same. It's a positive feedback loop, and the more you feed it, the more powerful the positive momentum you'll experience.

Gratitude Exercises

1. The gratitude game

This is game that I love to play daily and involve people I know.

It starts with 'Give me five things you are grateful for right now.' You are challenging that person to think of five random things that they can be grateful for. Allow me to give you some examples.

I'm grateful for:
-   my hairbrush
-   the brakes of my car
-   my lipstick
-   this pen on my desk
-   my thumbs
-   my chemistry teacher in school
-   my TV remote control
-   the soles of my winter boots

Another way of asking this question is 'What could you be grateful for right now?' This gently encourages the mind to look for things to be grateful for.

If you ask your friends and family what they are grateful for they will probably answer some of the following:

-   my life
-   my family
-   my job
-   my car
-   my house
-   my health

After this, they will struggle.

How do I know this? Every single group I have ever addressed and asked that same question has normally produced these answers. Unfortunately, we are not usually taught the Attitude of Gratitude.

Imagine the Attitude of Gratitude to be a giant new lens through which you can look at your life, providing you with greater richness of detail and colour. Certain elements that you are currently missing in your line of sight will suddenly come into view.

TIP: When you're looking for things to be grateful for, be like a child. Be curious like a child in your attitude. You could come up with being grateful for the keyboard on your computer, the glass holding your water, your nostrils or the four legs of the chair you're sitting on! Joking aside, when you start to focus on the little things in life, it's akin to taking your blinkers off and "seeing all around myself for the very first time," as someone remarked to me recently. Another person passionately expressed that it was like seeing life in colour rather than black and white.

2. Start a gratitude journal

It doesn't have to take more than a few minutes every evening, but writing down three or four things that went well that day (they can be really small-fry – a cheerful chat with a neighbour, a cuddle with your child, a delicious coffee) can have a profound impact on your happiness level. Numerous studies show that the simple act of spending fifteen minutes a day on this can significantly increase life satisfaction, reduce depressive symptoms and even improve sleep quality. Try it before bed (keep a notebook on your bedside table).

An unexpected benefit of this is that it will show you the things that really bring you joy (and, by implication, also those which don't).

It might feel a little artificial at first, so here's a list of ideas to get you started:

✓ Clean sheets on my bed
✓ Enough money to pay the bills
✓ Coffee in my favourite café
✓ Homemade soup that turned out well

✓ A houseplant that's thriving
✓ Singing loudly in the car
✓ A life-affirming conversation
✓ A child's nonsensical joke: 'Knock knock!' 'Who's there?'
   'Spoon.' 'Spoon who?' 'RED SPOON! Ha ha ha!'
✓ A thoughtful 'How are you?' text from a friend
✓ A self-seeded plant in my garden
✓ A perfectly crispy-skinned baked potato with butter on a
   cold night
✓ A square of delicious chocolate from the fridge
✓ An unprompted cup of tea arriving on my desk at the perfect
   moment
✓ An unexpected sunny spell
✓ Walking outside, whatever the weather
✓ Holding my partner's hand
✓ New shoes that don't rub
✓ Noticing a lovely smell: a rainy forest path, roast chicken,
   homemade cake
✓ A friendly bus driver
✓ A family hug
✓ Putting my pyjamas on early

- ✓ A bonfire
- ✓ Picking flowers
- ✓ Throwing sticks for a dog
- ✓ The local gym being so close to my house
- ✓ Good feedback for my work
- ✓ Swimming in the sea or a river and spotting a fish or a kingfisher on the way
- ✓ A brief chat with a friendly stranger on a train

3. Go deep

For the Attitude of Gratitude to really take hold, it's important to dig beneath the surface – to think more deeply about gratitude, consciously acknowledging everything that's going right for you. So at first, you may be thinking, "I'm grateful for my parents, my house, my dog…", but go deeper than that and be grateful for the door of your house. Be grateful for the person who made the keys that fit the lock to your front door. Be grateful for the privacy that closing the door affords. Be grateful for the lighting in your kitchen, or the roof above your head. Be grateful for the pen that you are using, because without it you wouldn't be able to write. Be grateful for the person who taught you to write. Work backwards and delve deeper into things. Challenge yourself.

4. Five ways to channel the Attitude of Gratitude

Thank other people. Whether it's acknowledging a colleague's help or a friend's thoughtfulness, or thanking your partner for loading the dishwasher, taking time out to express your gratitude means everybody benefits.

Think mindfully. Often we get so caught up in big-picture worries and problem-solving that we miss the joyful things in front of us. When you find yourself spiralling down a 'What if…?' worry trail, pull your attention back to the moment. What is it about where you are now that's worth appreciating?

Aim to be a radiator rather than a drainer. We all fall into one of these two camps. Negative people often seem to suck the air out of a room. If you make it your habit to answer positively when somebody asks you a question, that's a good start. Some people can in particular can get into a habit of self-deprecation, thinking it makes them appear more likeable and less arrogant if they subtly undermine themselves. But it can have the opposite effect. Positive vibes flow from positive people and an Attitude of Gratitude and positivity makes you magnetic.

Accept compliments graciously, with a simple 'thank you,' rather than a self-deprecating brush-off. If you counter a heartfelt compliment with a variation on 'this old thing!', it devalues the other person's kindness and opinion.

Remember gratitude is a numbers game. Practising grateful thought habits will bring your negative thoughts frequency down. It does this quite literally from moment to moment. When you have a positive thought in your head, you won't be able to focus on a negative one as it's impossible to think two thoughts simultaneously. Fill your head with the good stuff.

5. GOOD morning

People have often asked me what the best time of the day is to practise the Attitude of Gratitude. I always reply, 'Anytime.' However, it is my firm belief that gratitude is very advantageous to you first thing in the morning. It ultimately sets the tone of the day. The energy associated with a grateful heart is incomparable. Do you know anyone who is truly grateful for their life and everything it gives them?

So, why not ask yourself five things you are grateful for first thing in the morning whilst you are brushing your teeth? You have no excuse now!

13

The Road Ahead I Create

'Values offer focus amidst the chaos.'
~ Glenn C Stewart

What, in your mind, is the definition of 'values'?

They can be defined as what is important to oneself for optimal happiness and well-being. When we live in accordance with all our most important values, we can say we really are our best self.

Considering the fact that our core values in life underpin every action we take and decision we make, it's shocking how many of us never really stop to think about what our particular values are.

Imagine our life is a car. We have control of the steering wheel. The road ahead represents our values. The road we choose to follow will determine how our life journey progresses. Our values change over time, as we explore paths in our life. Some things which were important to us when we were 20 years old, such as staying up until 6 a.m. at a nightclub, have less importance when we are 45 years old. Usually!

In my work with clients, I'm often surprised by people's response to the request, "Tell me what your values are." It's not unusual for somebody to respond by saying, "Home, job, family." But these aren't your actual values – although they are aspects of life that are all impacted and shaped by your values. Many of the values that determine your priorities and perspective, shaping your behaviour, may not be conscious. As a result, they might not be immediately obvious to you. But if you're serious about letting go, you will need to take time to identify and unpick them and think about to what extent your life – your career, relationships and life situation – is playing out in accordance with them.

When you come to think about your values, you might start to question where they've come from and how well they serve you. Often the values we'd like to live by (for example, creativity, adventure and spontaneity) are a world away from the ones we find ourselves living by (safety, industry and control). This disharmony can create a deeply troubling sense of dissatisfaction, whatever the unique characteristics of the mismatch. If you struggle to put your finger on why you feel your life is on the wrong path, it's likely to be a consequence of this disconnect.

When I was growing up, my family moved to a valley with rolling hills and undulating roads. Within weeks of relocating to our new house, my parents made a decision for me which contributed to how I looked at life forever. They sold my bike. I was 10 years old.

The overall feeling that I experienced immediately was sadness at the subsequent lack of freedom. I still remember that feeling of loss as I saw my Raleigh bike being taken away. My parents' argument at the time was the potential danger of riding a bike in a hilly area. They deemed it too much of a risk. Even though other children in the area had bikes, the 'safety first' value which was high on my parents' agenda took precedence. This is an example of how values can influence decisions.

The event was a contributory factor which, combined with others, has led me to prize a sense of freedom as one of my core values. Later on in life, when I worked as an optometrist, I became self-employed and moved extensively around the UK. Today, I travel a great deal with my work as a coach and speaker. This is a reflection of my love of freedom and what it gives me: happiness and joy. Therefore anything which reduces my immediate sense of freedom causes me to feel uneasy and uncomfortable.

So, how can you get greater clarity on your own values? This simple exercise should help.

Exercise 1

Values deduction. Go to the list of values on pages 205–207. Examine the list. You can even photocopy it. Take your time to identify the ones that are really important to you. What I would suggest is to initially circle 40 which resonate with you on some level. Then narrow it down to 20 two days later, then finally to just 10 two days after that. Allowing some time between each review of your values will give you a greater sense of perspective and clarity. This exercise will enable you to drill down to identify what you truly regard as important.

Now look again at the original list in the book with all the values on it and ask yourself: which of them are you actually living by at the moment? Create a list of these. They may well stand in stark contrast to your list of core values. Pause to consider the impact of this on your motivation, confidence, well-being and sense of life-satisfaction.

Now write down a list of negative values that you think that you are following currently. These could be avoidance, safety, security, procrastination and self-sabotage. Being aware of your negative values is the first step towards letting go and changing them.

If you are a deeply creative person with a passion for the arts, but you're working long hours in a repetitive, analytical job that doesn't nurture this side of your personality and leaves very little time for creativity outside of work, you're stifling one of the values most central to your identity. Over a period of time, the impact of this is that you repeatedly undermine the very essence of who you are.

This is not to say you should jack in your job (although sometimes that might form part of the answer), but by understanding that you need to live in a way that allows your creativity to thrive, you can reassess your approach to work and life as a whole. It's really important that you don't ignore these signs, and that you take action to reset the balance. If your life values are not being met, your life will be travelling in a direction that leaves you feeling displaced. You will continue to feel a lot of frustration about your unmet needs, as you can't just override them.

You may try ignoring them, justifying this with a series of 'good sense' excuses: "I'm a grown up and I just have to get my head down and pay the mortgage", "There will be plenty of time for painting when I'm retired", "Most people hate their day-job", etc. Some of these excuses are persuasive. They sound sensible and mature. But don't be deceived. Mental health problems such as depression and anxiety are common side effects of ignoring what's really important to you deep down inside. And even if the fallout doesn't take the form of a clinical problem, there will be an element of sadness, of resentment, of having given up on the things that really matter to you.

I'll give you a few examples from my work with clients.

Case study

Sam

Sam came to me a few years ago for help. He was a very successful and wealthy entrepreneur. Sam had one daughter, who was ten at the time, and who lived with him every other weekend as he was divorced: a consequence of the fact that he had been a workaholic for years and never made time for his family. He had also gained weight, and often felt depressed because of this. During one of the sessions, I asked him to tell me which values were important to him. He wrote down on the flip chart the following:

'Success, travel, money, fun... Sophie [his daughter]'

Suddenly, he stopped himself and said, "Actually, can I put Sophie at the top of the list?"

It was revealing – clearly, his priorities were elsewhere. This simple response indicated to Sam where he was going wrong, and why he was unhappy.

He immediately realised that his happiness and joy came from spending more time with his daughter. However, he confessed that even then he was often distracted by work and that he sometimes had to cancel weekends he had planned with her, because of work commitments.

He then said, "I need to put my daughter first."

It was so simple, and yet he hadn't seen it until this point.

Exercise 2

What's liberating about this simple exercise is that it gives you a powerful insight into the thinking that's going on behind the scenes. Often, until something happens to force us to question our values, we bumble through life, being led by them blindly.

With clients, part of the 'penny drop' power comes from verbalising your values aloud and having them heard. But as you will be doing this exercise alone, try simply speaking them aloud to yourself. It might sound strange, but there's something about the act of speaking something that makes it easier to feel its power and authenticity than if you simply wrote it down.

Then ask yourself what you need to do to live your life according to your values. Say "I need to..." Then say out loud whatever it is that follows in your mind.

Deep within you there resides considerable intuitive wisdom: an instinctive understanding of what it is that you need in life. Think of it as a healthy craving – your heart's way of telling you what it is that you need in order to feel balanced and fulfilled.

If you're out of the habit of tuning into this wisdom, it can take a while for your more conscious 'ought to'/'have to' mindset to quieten down enough to enable you to hear what's going on underneath. Particularly if you're in the midst of a stressful period at work, or working through a challenging time in your personal life, your deep needs can feel like more of a luxury than a necessity, easy to ignore and override.

Case study

Martin

Let's take the example of a client: Martin, a doctor. He worked long hours as a GP, a job that sat with well with one of his core values: to make a difference. Despite the considerable stress, he felt he was able to serve his patients, which gave him a certain degree of satisfaction. Martin is also a father of two, so has little free time outside of work. He had another core value that he had latterly opted to ignore: a love of adventure. When he was a student and before he was a father, Martin went climbing every week. He was also a keen road cyclist. He completed a number of major challenges for the pure joy of training and the sense of achievement he got from them. These included climbing to the base camp of Mount Everest and completing an *étape* of the Tour de France.

Ten years into his career, he had totally given up on these passions. He cycled to work, but aside from that, those memories of scaling summits were hazy. Martin came to see me because he was feeling flat and he didn't know why. It was making him doubt everything about his life. He was wondering whether he was having a mid-life crisis; whether he should leave his wife, or change career.

"I have everything I've ever wanted: a good job, a lovely family, somewhere nice to live, enough money... But I don't feel happy. It's as if there's something important missing, but I can't work out for the life of me what it is."

We ran thorough the list of values and came to the conclusion that his top three were: Purpose, Adventure and Connection. We talked about what he had loved about the expeditions and adventures of his past. In part, he loved them because they enabled him to foster deep friendships with his teammates and companions. There was a social benefit to his cycling and climbing as well as a physical and emotional benefit.

He had abandoned this aspect of his life because it seemed to make sense practically: he was time poor, and had to focus on the 'have to's. But in doing so, he'd compromised on something that was far more than just a hobby.

We began to look at ways he could integrate adventure into his life in micro-doses. He used the rides to work as sessions where he could get fit in training for a race – his first in almost a decade. He also booked a camping holiday in the Alps with his family, and bought a hiking backpack to carry his toddler so the whole family could go walking.

As a result of these changes, he began to feel his life was returning to a course he felt more comfortable with. He was finally back in the driving seat.

When you love doing what you're doing, you're naturally focused. With a clear end goal that is in keeping with the things that matter most to you, you're less likely to get distracted and to lack motivation or energy. In contrast, when you feel as if you've sleep-walked into a career or situation, you feel out of sorts with it. This impacts on your productivity: you may drift a little and you're more likely to fall prey to the temptations of social media. You don't value your own time enough, whether this manifests as being overgenerous with it and offering other people support and assistance to the detriment of the things on your own 'to do' list, or wasting time procrastinating online. It's an easy habit to fall into, and a hard one to break, but if you find yourself doing too much of this, you need to get back in touch with your own core values and think about the changes you could make in your life that would make you feel more in control.

If you examine your life, looking at the different areas of relationships, family, health, career and fun, which of your values do you think are serving you and which are not? For example, your dream is to leave your job at the bank and open your own coffee shop. However, you never seem to take the first step of researching how to open your own place. Your need for security (one of your highest values) stops you from doing this.

An unfocused mind is one that constantly seeks distraction. Like a toddler bingeing on sweets, it will latch onto anything that gives it a little 'hit' of information or stimulation. A new text or email, checking Instagram and Facebook, messaging a friend to ask what they're up to tomorrow. As the modern world provides such varied, readily available temptations at all times, it takes a degree of wilfully blinkered focus to shut it out. Frankly, unless you have a strong sense of your core values, the bigger picture can easily fall by the wayside. Distraction is the enemy of productivity, after all. It's important to fight it, otherwise you'll end up years down the line, having lost all sense of where you wanted to be.

One thing to remember is that values can and do change over time. Allow me to explain further.

A good friend of mine, Nick, moved from Scotland to Wales and settled down in Cardiff with his girlfriend. He had absolutely no interest in or intention of learning to drive. He was quite happy and content with his partner driving him instead. After four years of living in Cardiff, Nick started driving lessons and, within months, passed his driving test. What do you think the reason behind his sudden change of heart was?

His values had changed. Whereas once upon a time there had been just the two of them, Nick now had two young children. As they needed to be transported from place to place, he now had to take responsibility. Nick readily acknowledged that 'responsibility' was once not one of his core values. Fatherhood had changed this.

What I recommend you do is to 'check in' with your values using the values deduction exercise above every four to six months to gauge where your mind is focused.

Here's a common example:

Mr and Mrs Edwards had been married for 25 years. Their children had grown up and become successful professionals in the fields of medicine and law. On the surface, to the outside world, everything was perfect with the Edwards' marriage. However, one spring day the Edwards announced to friends and family that they were getting divorced. There was no adultery, nor any money issues. What was the reason, therefore, that the Edwards had decided to split up?

It's a story which is commonplace in society. When asked by friends why they were separating, Mr Edwards replied, "We live separate lives, and have stayed together for the sake of the children for too long. We have drifted apart." Mrs Edwards commented: "I don't recognise him any more. He lives an adventurous outdoor life with his friends, while I prefer the indoors more. We have just grown apart."

Imagine the values of each of the couple to be represented by a road. Initially in their marriage, the two roads were parallel. However, somewhere along the line, the roads started to diverge. Over the years, a stage is reached where the Edwards were so far apart on their life journey that they no longer had much left in common. The roads had visibly moved in different directions.

 TIP: The lesson to be learnt here is that it is important to revisit your values periodically as mentioned above. Hindsight is a powerful process. Paying attention to your current core values can be an even more valuable lesson.

Self-Value and Building It Up

On a scale from 1 to 10 (1 = low, 10 = high), how much do you value yourself?

How an individual acts in any situation can be related to how they value themself. For example, have you noticed that some people tend to deflect a compliment that is directed their way? They will reply to a positive comment about their cardigan with words such as "This old thing!" or "Yeah, right!" A friend may even call you on the phone for a chat and say the words, "It's only me…" When you truly value yourself, this vocabulary would not even cross your mind. Think of someone you know who really values themself and is subsequently confident. Notice the positive language they use, as opposed to the examples above.

Exercise 3

The next time someone pays you a compliment, just say a simple 'Thank you'. There is no need to return a compliment just because of a sense of obligation. If you deflect or negate a compliment then who are you disrespecting? Two people. The person who paid you the compliment, and yourself. A genuine compliment is a form of love, admiration and respect at the deepest level.

The Subject of People-Pleasers

I recently gave a talk to some entrepreneurs and asked the audience if there were any people-pleasers in the house. Over half the audience raised their hands.

Look at people-pleasing as a strategy. Of course, acts of altruism and helping others are important for human relationships and forming deep connections.

It can be seen as a strategy to gain love and acceptance from others. Almost every self-confessed people-pleaser has admitted that at times it can be exhausting, yet they find it difficult to help themselves. They find it challenging to say 'no', and feel guilt and fear if they do. This is the fear of upsetting anyone and not being liked. On the flip side are the benefits of being rewarded with being liked and loved. Essentially, people-pleasers are receiving a form of external appreciation. The twin rewards of being liked whilst simultaneously avoiding any negative feelings themselves is subconsciously a very attractive proposition. At the deepest level, the people-pleaser is not valuing their own time or energy. Because of the positive reinforcement, over time this becomes a habit. However, it can lead to resentment, frustration and exhaustion for the people-pleaser.

Exercise 4

Unfortunately there will be people who start to devalue your time and energy. Unless you take considered action and start to guard your time and energy, life could get very difficult. What do you stand to gain if you let go of saying 'yes' as frequently as you currently do, and introduce the word 'no' more often?

What are the two most valuable resources that we have? The answer is quite simple: time and energy. Time is something we cannot get back, while energy we have to replenish through sleep, rest and recovery. Time wasters and energy vampires can drain us of both. Even though people don't necessarily want to waste your most valuable resources, it still happens – if you allow it. That choice can be brought to a conscious level by a very powerful daily one-word reminder: RUTHLESS.

I remember telling someone to put the word RUTHLESS on a post-it note on their bedroom and bathroom walls. I was met with initial disbelief, as she recognised the word only from a negative perspective. In truth, I explained it was a reminder to her not to waste time or energy on the things which did not serve her. When I saw her two weeks later, she commented on how much time and energy she had preserved due to seeing this powerful daily reminder. The upshot had been that she no longer accepted every social invitation, she went to bed earlier instead of watching too much television, and had therefore been having much better-quality sleep. This had improved her mood in the office and she felt she could concentrate on work tasks for longer and her retention of facts was heightened.

Look at RUTHLESS as a reminder to protect your time and energy.

Exercise 5

The way we speak to ourself forms our own personal reality. If we constantly berate ourself, downgrade our chances for success or deny ourself happiness, then that becomes our truth. In order to combat our usual negative thinking and feelings, here are three simple yet disruptive thoughts in the form of affirmations. Repeat them daily. The most effective way of introducing this into your day is when you are brushing your teeth first thing in the morning. As you look into the mirror, repeat the words.

'I love you.
I value you.
I respect you.'

The new daily dialogue does not necessarily have to be spoken out loud if that's inconvenient. What's actually more important is the repetitive element. The words will slowly infuse into your subconscious mind and become accepted over time. Be wary that the voice of doubt and uncertainty may appear out of the blue. Just observe it, while continuing to recite the words. Personally, I recommend you to keep reciting them for approximately 100 days. You can even teach them to friends and family who you think are open to change.

Exercise 6

Often we can let life slip by, and forget what made us happy in the first place. By letting go of apathy and procrastination and valuing what us makes us feel alive, we can again move towards a place of happiness. Many pleasurable activities and hobbies which once gave us joy are 'put on the shelf' or kept 'for a rainy day' as we prioritise what we think is important at that time.

What activity did you use to really enjoy doing, but no longer do? Perhaps horse riding, tenpin bowling, reading, walking, going to the cinema, travelling, meeting friends for coffee? Set a plan in action to try it again, within the next three months.

In the grand scheme of time, our life is short, but invaluable. We may as well value it, and enjoy doing the things we love. This is a reminder to reconnect to something that you may once have loved, but which has fallen by the wayside.

14

Letting Go of Negative Thoughts

'Don't believe everything you think.'
~ Allan Lokos

'What if...?' can be one of the most disempowering thoughts, launching you into a whirlpool of negativity.

Worry and therefore anxiety is primarily based in the future. As our thoughts are directed to events and situations that have not happened yet, our imagination will start to create a mini movie. This mini movie of future events will then evoke feelings and emotions within us.

These feelings can sway between excitement and concern. When the feelings are weighted towards concern, we start to worry. As our overthinking escalates, this can lead to us visualising worst-case scenarios and what psychologists call 'catastrophe thinking'.

Scenario 1

Imagine that you are on a train. You are calm, happy and enjoying your music. As the train pulls out of the latest station, a text message from your dad informs you of some bad news. Your mum has been involved in an accident. You call immediately but can't get through. Mobile phone signal is poor. Immediately your mind starts to create 'What if...?' scenarios and soon you are in a state of panic. You feel your heart racing, your breathing is laboured and your head starts to spin. 'What if...?'

The physiological symptoms of anxiety are real. Our thoughts are real. However, think back to a time when you were worried, and ended up realising that it wasn't as bad as you thought. In this instance, you find out that your mum is perfectly fine, as a motorcyclist has hit her car from behind. Suddenly all the fears and emotions that you were feeling disappear.

Our mind can rapidly focus on what we don't want to happen, or what we perceive is going to happen, even if we have no evidence of it happening. A high proportion of most people's daily thoughts are negative and disempowering.

One of the mind's primary functions is to keep you safe. It is its 'safety first' perspective on life that causes it to rapidly switch gears to certainty and safety mode. It's as if the mind is an expert at delivering worst-case scenarios.

What would happen if you could let go of overthinking, and started to focus more on the present? It's not easy, but it's definitely worthwhile.

As mentioned in Chapter 2: 'Your Blueprint', most of our thinking is automated. We are largely living life on autopilot. Here are some scenarios where that autopilot can kick in and we can end up overthinking in the workplace:

- worry you'll make a mistake during your first day in a new job
- worry you're a fraud and will be found out (psychologists term this 'imposter syndrome')
- worry you'll sound stupid in a meeting
- worry you're going to miss a deadline
- worry your colleague doesn't like you

If we let things get to the point where we're lying in bed worrying at night, it can affect our sleep pattern, and soon we can be categorised as an insomniac – an estimated one third of people in the UK suffer from insomnia.

How many times have you been in a situation yourself where, because of overthinking, you worried yourself into an anxious state? You may have been in the shower at home, reflecting on the day, and suddenly you started overthinking. You could have been overthinking just before you entered a cinema. Whilst the movie was playing, you were sitting there in silence paying no attention to the plot. You were too busy worrying.

Take a look at this diagram.

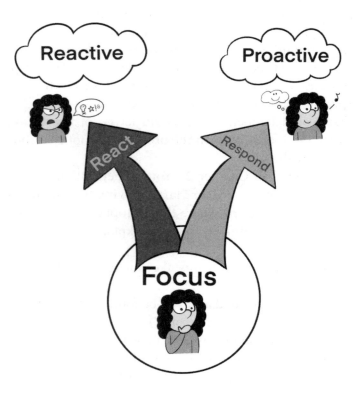

The diagram illustrates the mind's ability to choose between being reactive and proactive. For example, you may be thinking of applying for a new job. Your friend, who's focused on safety and has a low-risk strategy attitude in life, attempts to dissuade you from this. They spell out the reasons for 'Better the devil you know'.

 TIP: It's a good idea to print a copy of the diagram to remind you that we can be reactive or proactive.

So how can we let go of our overthinking, or more specifically our negative overthinking?

Research has suggested that the prefrontal cortex, the brain's executive centre which governs intellectual activity, is interconnected with the emotional centre, the amygdala. We can therefore influence our emotion-producing amygdala indirectly through observing and challenging our thoughts. The following tools and strategies can assist you in developing a more self-aware and resilient mindset.

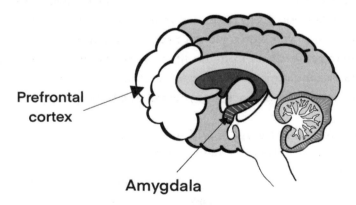

Prefrontal cortex

Amygdala

As you develop resilience and greater self-awareness, your ability to deal with negative thinking expands. Here are ten great techniques you can start using today.

1. Observe your thoughts

This can be achieved through quiet time and meditation. As Dr Richard Davidson has said, 'Meditation gives you the wherewithal to pause, observe how easily the mind can exaggerate the severity of a setback, and resist getting drawn into the abyss.' By stepping away from your thoughts, you are able to observe thoughts as 'things' and diminish their power over you. Remember, from the Blueprint Process in Chapter 2, that thinking produces feelings. Feelings will always arise. These cannot be stopped. You can, however, observe your thoughts and choose a different meaning for a thought.

Scenario 2

Imagine you've been told that you didn't get a promotion at work. The interview went well, but it was given to someone who you think is not as good as you. You start feeling rejected and angry. Stop. Observe your feelings. Now observe your negative thoughts. These are thoughts and feelings. They do not define you. Keep observing your thoughts. Instead of poring over 'why' you didn't get the promotion and feeling rejected, aim to get feedback from the interviewers, let go and learn from this disappointment, and plan for another promotion. Label this as a temporary setback, not yourself as a failure.

Observing your thoughts will give you time to *reframe* them positively, give them a new meaning, reduce emotion and regain control.

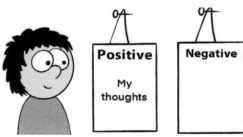

2. Challenge your thoughts

Have you ever had one negative thought which has just suddenly spiralled out of all proportion and out of control? You feel helpless and powerless. Thoughts can create feelings in milliseconds.

Start writing down on a piece of paper your current negative thoughts. Challenging these thoughts can create doubt as to their veracity. Once you start doubting your own negative thoughts, this will reduce their emotional charge. Ask yourself questions such as 'What could I be thinking which is not true?' and 'What conclusions am I jumping to?'

For example, you may not have heard from someone you've been on several romantic dates with after sending them a birthday gift and texting them a 'Happy Birthday' message. Within a couple of hours, you are jumping to conclusions and feeling emotional. Just remembering the Blueprint Process – Blueprint generates thoughts leading to feelings – can help return you to awareness.

3. Shorten Time Limit for Decisions

Sometimes we can overthink a decision. This can often be due to fear – for example, of making a mistake, of failure or of the past reoccurring. How many times have you ever made a decision and then wished you had trusted your gut instinct instead? By shortening the time within which we make a decision, we allow the instinctive part of us to influence the decision-making process. The longer we ruminate over an idea, a decision or a choice, the greater our chance of making the wrong decision. That's not to say that important decisions do not take time. It's just that the time spent considering could sometimes be more appropriately aligned with the level of importance of the decision. For example, whether you should go and mow the lawn can be decided in under 30 seconds, whilst whether you should put in an offer on a house might be considered in under 30 minutes.

4. Back to the Future (Thinking)!

Look back at your life five years ago. I'm betting that there are things that you used to worry about which now, looking back, feel ridiculous. Ask yourself, 'Is what I am thinking and worrying about right now going to matter in five years' time?' In the grand scheme of our lives, we often allow our worries to get out of proportion, subsequently leading to negative feelings and emotions. We allow our mind to build up a negative charge around a worry that we could let go of right now. Think of the worries that you have had in the past: what would have happened if you had let go of them immediately?

5. Movement

I have always found exercise time a great time to re-energise myself. Not only does exercise lower the stress hormone, cortisol, but it increases dopamine and serotonin levels, leaving us feeling good. When you feel good, your mind is not only clearer, but able to make faster and more accurate decisions based on logic rather than negative emotion.

Exercise in this context does not necessarily mean attending a gym – it can be any activity you enjoy, such as walking, running, cycling, rowing, climbing or tennis. Just taking action is the first step to helping your mental and emotional mindset.

6. Control

Refer back to the Power Statement 'You can't control what you can't change, and you can't change what you can't control.' When we accept that we don't and can't control everything, it's as if a weight is lifted off our shoulders. Think of situations where you feel you need to be in control. Imagine that you let go of that need. How do you feel? The need to be in control is the foundation for a great deal of overthinking. Time to let it go?

7. SIMPLE

Write the word 'SIMPLE' on a post-it note and keep it in a prominent place. 'I'm really quite simple. I plant flowers and watch them grow... I stay at home and watch the river flow,' sang George Harrison. Overthinking involves overcomplicating problems and creating new ones as a result. Can you imagine looking through a lens of simplicity instead? How would it encourage you to change your attitude towards problem-solving and handling important issues? How would it improve your clarity and speed of thought in decision-making? As you develop an attitude of simplicity, it starts to influence all that you do. Keep life simple...

8. Ruthless

Refer to the RUTHLESS segment in Chapter 13, 'The Road Ahead I Create'.

9. STOP

Self-awareness is key to letting go of negative thinking. As you train yourself to become aware that you are thinking negatively, say the word 'STOP' to yourself. This will interrupt your negative chain of thinking and bring you back into the moment. If you are going through an overthinking period in your life, try this neat reminder. Write the word 'STOP' between your thumb and index finger on your left hand if you are right-handed, and vice versa. Even glancing at this momentarily through the day can have the effect of disrupting your chain of thought. By doing this repeatedly over a 100-day period, it can form the habit of interrupting your negative thought patterns. As you let go of these negative thoughts more rapidly, you start to feel more present and in the moment.

10. Set Daily Reminders

Smart technology has been criticised for bringing an information overload into our lives. This information overload can corrupt our thinking, causing us to feel stressed, anxious and overwhelmed. However, we can use smart technology to our advantage. One highly effective way of reminding yourself is using the smartphone alarm or reminder system. You can set your smartphone to remind you to do any of the nine strategies listed above (or indeed anything that you have felt to be helpful in this book) at particular times of the day. We often lead busy lives; so busy that we can easily forget to follow any productive techniques to assist us. Therefore it is very easy to 'slip', as a few of my clients have attested over the years. Personally, I believe that when you think everything is going well, that is the most important time to ensure that you have your electronic reminders in place. These will gently remind you to stay focused and on track.

15

Advancing the
Letting Go Process

'Have patience. All things are difficult
before they become easy.'
~ Saadi

What is the most important conversation that you will have
daily? It is the one that you have with yourself. Unfortunately,
we have an abundance of external influences which carve
out a space in our thinking time. The *Let It Go* philosophy
is important in maintaining your healthy mindset. Here are
six proven ways to advance your life by letting go. Each step
increases your awareness and involves taking action. The
benefits to you can be immeasurable, and those around you
will feel the ripple effect. Read through this chapter and see
which of the six practical methods described resonates most
with you. Make a decision to start acting on it within 24 hours.
This will give you a sense of forward momentum and progress.

1. The Average of Five

If we examine our life, we are typically connected with people
everywhere. Traditionally, it was people who lived in our
vicinity, who we worked with and saw on a regular basis. Now,
as the world becomes heavily interconnected via technology

and social media, we have interactions with people who we have never actually physically met. Our life can now be influenced by a menu of multiple social choices.

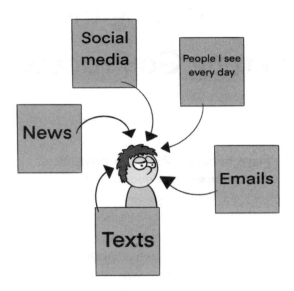

It was suggested originally by Jim Rohn that our happiness depends on who we are most commonly communicating with at the time – an average of five people. Social psychologist Dr David McClelland of Harvard says that "the people you habitually associate with determine as much as 95 percent of your success or failure in life." This is a profound thought.

It then follows that if our primary influencers are those who we communicate with constantly, this will now include who we text message, Skype, email, contact on social media and speak to on the phone.

Who are the top five people that you communicate with on a weekly basis? When I have conducted this exercise with groups, they have often been surprised and shocked when they become aware of their direct influencers. This is not something we tend to think about, as we are often on autopilot.

Case study

Amanda

I remember an interesting email from an entrepreneurial client. This was a month after she had carried out the Average of Five Evaluation exercise. She had just let go of a group of three friends that she had associated with for four years previously. This had seemed to her husband a little dramatic at the time! However, she had realised through the exercise that the ex-friends had been a highly toxic group of people who had left her feeling negative, frustrated and disempowered every time they had met up for coffee on a Friday. She discovered that she had stayed with this group because of the fear of being alone and of not being able to make new friends. She now looks back on these fears as completely unfounded as she has made new entrepreneurial friends, more aligned with her values of support, contribution and encouragement. The following exercise had made her aware for the first time of the influential power that other people had on her own happiness and success.

Exercise 1

1. Think of the top five people that you communicate with on a weekly basis. This communication can be:
   - face to face
   - telephone
   - text message or email
   - Skype or equivalent
   - social media
2. Write down their first names.
3. Put a tick next to their name if they leave you empowered with their presence in your life, a cross if they are disempowering

or a tick and a cross if they both empower and disempower you at different times.

This is primarily an awareness tool to give you leverage if you are looking for areas that you need to change. Sometimes someone will ask what happens when family are named in the list. As mentioned previously, the only thing that you can do is limit the time spent with family influences which adversely affect you!

2. The Backpack

You may have heard people say, 'I feel weighed down by...' We can often identify with this feeling of physically being weighed down by something that's on our mind. It could also be something from the past. Imagine that you are carrying a backpack with all the rubbish that consumes and weighs you down. It could be a feeling that you have carried for a few days, or even for years. It feels heavy, and starts to affect your posture. Wouldn't it be good just to put it down? Try this powerful visualisation exercise of putting down your mental and emotional backpack. It's a tool that you can perform in minutes, and which will give you an immediate feeling of relaxation.

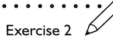

Exercise 2

1. Stand with your feet hip-width apart. Imagine you are carrying a backpack, and put your body into the position it would be in if that backpack was very heavy. Notice your posture, with your shoulders and back slightly bent over. This is what actually happens when we feel 'weighed down'.
2. Now close your eyes.
3. Imagine that you can now unclip the backpack and release it behind you. Perform this part as if you are actually taking it off – this enhances the process for you.
4. Now stand up straight and take a single step forward, as if you have just let go of the backpack.
5. Now imagine the backpack is dissolving away behind you.
6. Take a deep breath and imagine feeling lighter and free.
7. Shake your arms down by your sides, and take another deep breath.
8. Smile, and open your eyes.

The powerful process of visualising the actual physical act of letting go of the backpack will help you daily to let go of negative baggage that you could be carrying that day.

The best times to let go of the mental backpack are first thing in the morning, lunchtime and early evening after a busy day. However, you may wish to carry out the backpack technique at any time when you feel someone else has directly left you feeling drained or negative. This could be after a telephone call or a face-to-face interaction.

3. The Letter

"David, the art of letter writing is all but dead." Someone I once knew told me this. I thought about it momentarily, and agreed. When was the last time that you wrote a handwritten letter, placed it in an envelope and posted it with a real stamp? Think of someone in your life that you would love to surprise with a handwritten note. Their amazed face as they received your note would be priceless. Imagine that you receive a handwritten note today. The chances are, you would keep it, as it is a thing of rarity. We don't even send birthday cards with any frequency any more. These days we are reminded by social media that it's a friend's birthday, and are given a menu of pre-populated choices of how to convey our greeting to them.

Sending a letter to someone could involve forgiveness. Often things that have happened in the past but which we haven't let go of can, like an insidious virus, consume us from within. The simple yet powerful act of a forgiving letter can immediately relieve you of a longstanding reservoir of resentment and negativity. We may have something that we would like to conclude, that we can't seem to shake, and perhaps a letter would be the best way to put things in perspective. Have you heard of someone sending an email or text, and what they were trying to say was lost in translation?

Case studies

Grant

Back in 2015, a business client had been having marital problems. His wife had had fears about his commitment to her in their marriage. He was constantly at work, in meetings or away on business. He readily admitted that he had lost his way. The state of the marriage had left her feeling vulnerable and insecure.

He sent a handwritten letter expressing his love and gratitude to her. When she received his handwritten letter – which was, incidentally, posted to their own address – she was elated. It wasn't just the letter, she later confessed, which made her smile. It was what the letter represented. It represented the effort and time that he had taken to write and post it. The letter was part of a series of actions that my client took to improve his relationship with his wife.

Marcia

I received a text from a previous workshop attendee. She had written a letter to an old friend who she thought was not valuing the friendship. The letter had been received by her friend with surprise and shock. Her friend arranged a meet-up and the two cleared the air. The friend apologised and admitted that perhaps she had been consumed with her own 'negative stuff' and had lost sight of their friendship.

Exercise 3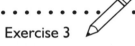

You will need a pen, paper, envelope and postage stamp for this exercise.

Who could you write a letter to? Someone who is in your life? It could be someone from the past who you would like to thank or convey forgiveness to. Often we feel things need to be resolved, yet we don't particularly want to physically see that person.

Perhaps you could write a letter to a loved one, just to gently remind them that they are loved? I have even personally heard of someone who sent a letter to someone who is deceased. The envelope was left unaddressed but the letter was still posted. The act itself was, to the sender, a cathartic moment in the process of letting go.

4. The Soundtrack of Your Life

I used to label myself as 'not a morning person'. I would wake, groan and make a concerted attempt to start the mental machinery. Our mood first thing in the morning can be enhanced by music. As we wake up, our energy level may be low as our body has been mainly motionless for (typically) 6–8 hours. A simple yet effective technique that I have practised over the years is to compile a music playlist – my morning playlist. This playlist is specifically of tracks I find energising.

Remember that music is pure energy, just as you are. If you hear a sad piece of music, then this can lower your mood. Conversely, if you play upbeat music, this can change your mood in an uplifting way. Think of a song right now that makes you feel good. The vibration of that song can cheer you up instantly. Just the act of listening to 'feel-good' music can change your morning and change your day.

We need to give ourself every little edge which is going to assist us in being more in charge of our mind, actions and life. If you currently do this, then great. If not, then investing a little time to set a playlist up will be worthwhile.

Follow the exercise below to change your morning mindset, and let go of negative moods.

Exercise 4

1. Compile a selection of your top 30–40 empowering, upbeat songs
2. Store them on your phone or electronic device of choice.
3. Play them as soon as you wake up, in the bathroom, over breakfast, or on the way to work.
4. We can make multiple playlists over the months to satisfy our need for variety.

5. Out of Sight, Out of Mind!

Look around you. That might mean your car, your office, your wardrobe or your home. Let's look at our wardrobe first. As with mental baggage, we will often keep unwanted things in our wardrobe. There are a multitude of reasons why we keep clothes for longer than we need. These may include sentimental reasons, fear of missing out ("I may want to wear it at a later date"), guilt (for example, you feel you have wasted money), thinking it'll come back into fashion, or apathy (you are just not monitoring your wardrobe space!).

Some questions that you can ask yourself include:

- Will I be wearing this within the next six months?
- Could I offer it to someone less fortunate than me, perhaps through a charity shop?
- Who do I know that will benefit from this?
- If I free the extra space up in my wardrobe, how will that help me?

Even the act of letting go of clothes and freeing up space in your wardrobe can have a liberating effect on you. That feeling of less claustrophobia and more space. This is reinforced by you actually seeing this first thing every morning. A good start to the day.

This practical technique also applies to many other aspects of our daily life.

I remember a friend's wife mentioning the state of the back of his car. It was a complete mess. She then went on to disclose that it was a source of stress to him. He would often be rifling through it in the morning, attempting to find something he needed for a business presentation that day, or something that he couldn't find in the house. He would often be heard saying 'It must be in the back of my car!'. You can imagine his chaotic mind first thing in the morning.

Often there is an area of our life which could be 'tidied up', helping to reduce our stress and anxiety. Think of when we suffer overwhelm. Little things such as being able to immediately find a document for a meeting, or the screwdriver for a table leg that needs tightening, can really assist in keeping stress levels low.

Exercise 5

Where in your life could you find time to clear up the clutter, create space and lighten your load? The second and perhaps more important step is: what could you do about it today? If that's not practical, then put a date in your diary, and follow through. Again, this is your choice – but you can start small. Even sorting out one drawer will feel like an achievement!

★ **TIP:** Take action and try one of the exercises in this chapter today. Don't leave it to tomorrow!

6. Attitude 24

The number 24 in Attitude 24 refers to 24 months. In two years' time, if you are doing what you are doing today, will this bring you what you want? Think of this question in terms of relationships, career, health and business. Here are some examples to think about:

- Waking up late
- Procrastinating
- Never taking time off

- People-pleasing
- Lacking self-care
- Not having enough sleep
- Starting projects but never finishing them
- Last-minute panic on work schedules
- Not replying in time to messages
- Lack of commitment to prearranged appointments/meetings
- Not looking after your appearance
- Always blaming, never taking responsibility
- Failing to keep promises
- Being disorganised
- Lack of planning

By answering the above question, you can take stock and make a decision. Choose a behaviour that you currently identify with (this may be one that isn't on the list), and then project two years into the future to see if it will assist in getting you to where you'd like to be. If your instinct is that things will not be any different in two years, then perhaps it's time to start letting go, and replace it with a more productive behaviour? As mentioned previously, habits take around 66 days to form, after daily practice.

The mental shift needed to start letting go of unproductive habits often requires advanced awareness of the possible consequences. We are perhaps aware that we are on autopilot and unintentionally sabotaging our own success. However, we appear to lack the motivation to change.

When the pain of losing out on your dreams is greater than your need to maintain an unproductive habit, you will move to make a change. Now start focusing on two years from now. What do you feel you need to let go of to move towards making your dreams reality?

Jim Rohn coined the Law of Diminishing Intent: 'The longer you wait to do something you should do now, the greater the odds that you will never actually do it.'

16

Five Rules to Live By

'Whether you are a success or failure in life has little
to do with your circumstances; it has much more
to do with your choices.'
~ Nido Qubein

I think it's important to keep in mind the following five principles. They're a good way to sense-check decisions and ensure you're living a life that's true to your values – the sort of life that you'll be able to look back on and honestly feel that you lived to the full.

Rule #1: Be REAL

In a world where many of us are consumed by the business of managing the public perception of ourselves via our digital alter egos, fakeness in all its forms can feel like an epidemic. Only those with the strongest sense of self and the thickest of skin are immune to the lure of airbrushing, editorialising and general tampering with personality, appearance and behaviour. It's not hard to see why: scrolling through a Facebook newsfeed can leave you feeling like that Bruce Springsteen line, 'Want to change my clothes, my face, my name...' Left unchecked, social media has the insidious power to turn us all into teenagers, stuck in an unpleasant hall of mirrors, constantly reminded to measure ourselves against everybody else. Most of the time, we find ourselves wanting. Everything becomes a competition.

We never feel good enough. We're constantly searching for the next thing to make us feel good about ourself. It's a constant treadmill of torment and frustration.

This is why being real feels more important than ever. Authenticity is the quality we crave. To be the kind of person who doesn't care what anyone else thinks. Who is comfortable in their own skin, knows that there are more important things in life than Instagram 'likes' and would never lie awake wondering what other people think of them.

When you set yourself a challenge to keep it real, the first step is to try to spot when you're going against the authenticity checklist. Here it is.

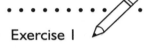

Exercise 1

In any situation where you are experiencing even a slight feeling of apprehension:

1. Are you doing what feels intuitively like the right thing at that moment?

2. Would you still choose to behave or react in the same way if nobody was watching?

Have you thought deeply about your values and priorities in life? Are you acting in accordance with these, in the way we discussed in Chapter 13?

Keeping it real is harder than it sounds. But when you do, it leaves you free to define your life the way you want to.

The Traits of Authentic Happy People

- **They don't seek attention.**
  When you have a strong internal sense of self-worth and confidence in who you are, you don't need to be bolstered constantly by other people.

- **They don't need to be liked.**
  Authenticity means knowing your own value – it isn't contingent on popularity. Authentic people genuinely believe this and therefore actually become even more attractive as a result of their inner confidence.
- **They're comfortable in their own skin.**
  They feel good about themselves, and know that longing to be more like anyone else is a total waste of time. As Oscar Wilde said, "Be yourself, as everyone else is taken."
- **They're straight talkers.**
  Even when a conversation is difficult, they'll say what needs to be said. They have an inner strength which gives them more influential power.
- **They don't show off or talk themselves down.**
  The need to feel significant in the eyes of others is not a priority. They see that as a waste of time.
- **They're consistent.**
  There's a phrase I think is really useful: what you do in one thing, you do in everything. This is truer of authentic people than anyone else. They know who they are and they're confident in their values.
- **They have integrity.**
  They're true to their word. They don't say one thing and do another. It is one of their key values.
- **They don't need to have the last word.**
  It is unimportant for them to have to prove their point.
- **They don't have to prove people wrong.**
  They understand that attempting to prove someone else wrong at every opportunity is a huge sign of a lack of confidence in themselves and that this act also could lead to belittling the other person.
- **They are always looking to help others.**
  Genuine people try to help automatically in times of need.
- **They're interested in other people.**
  In conversations they are not trying to press their own agenda over the other person's.

- **They are not consumed with gossip.**
  Talking about other people in a derogatory or judgmental fashion is of no interest to them.

If you suffer from lack of confidence, this list may look alarmingly unrealistic to you. Perhaps you read it thinking: 'I worry a lot about what other people think of me; I self-deprecate all the time; I'm always looking at friends and colleagues wishing I was more like them...'

But intuitively, I'm betting you recognise that people who don't have a need to prove themselves to anyone else are the ones who appear most genuine. Let me give you a personal example to demonstrate this.

> Some years ago, a good friend of mine ran a Speed Dating night. Sometimes she'd ask her brother along to make up the numbers as there would be more women than men on a given night. Unlike the other men who were there, because he didn't have the anxiety of being there specifically to meet someone, he was at his most relaxed. He didn't feel he had anything to prove. As a result, his sister told him afterwards that a lot of the women who had been there were interested in him because he seemed genuine and relaxed!
>
> He was free to just be himself and 'be nice' – he wasn't trying to be cool, or conjure an appearance of success or cleverness.

Have you heard of anyone going for a job interview with a very relaxed attitude because they already had job offers elsewhere, or were not really interested in the job, yet ended up succeeding in the interview and being offered the job? The less you have riding on something, the more relaxed you are as a result.

The beauty of the letting go process is that it resets your internal framework, helping your brain to forge new, more secure and empowering default settings. You'll no longer feel the need to prove yourself to anyone. The faulty thinking that causes you to seek approval from elsewhere and triggers your toxic thinking settings can be rewired. The net result is that you'll find a new sense of self-acceptance and peace with yourself. This frees you up to become more authentic and far more resilient. With this new confidence and groundedness, you'll find yourself manifesting many of the genuine qualities listed above without really having to try.

The first step to change is awareness, and hopefully you should be more aware after reading this book of aspects of you that could be worked on and improved.

RULE #2: Be RUTHLESS

I've included this again in this chapter, as I feel it is very a useful point to remember in your daily rituals. Whenever I've taught this, it's been met with quizzical faces. 'Being ruthless' to most people conjures up images of stepping on other people's toes, gaining advantage at the expense of others or simply hurting someone else's feelings.

The reason I've recommended being ruthless has more to do with the attitude you adopt towards your own time and energy. Time and energy, as you may agree, are the two fundamental resources in our lives which we consume daily. The energy can be replenished, but the time won't come back.

How many times have you arrived at a social occasion and wished you hadn't bothered? How many times has your gut instinct warned you off going somewhere or starting something but you've ignored it, only to regret it later? Time is precious, yet we are prone to wasting it on a daily basis. It is known that more people are busy surfing social media these days than actually watching television in the United States. Do you know anyone who is engaged in unproductive relationships with friends who constantly take without contributing much to the relationship? Relationships like this can be draining of energy.

When you deeply value yourself, you understand how precious your time is and you understand that energy, too, is limited. You won't want to squander either of these things on negative people, or work late for a boss who doesn't treat you with respect. You won't want to waste an evening browsing trivial status updates online when you could be doing something that nurtures your spirit and recharges your energy (think reading a great book, talking to a close friend, exercising, or even going to bed early). Valuing yourself by valuing your time and energy is a game changer when you're looking at making positive changes your life.

Time is our most precious resource. The free time you have is yours to use as you wish, but because work and family life can be draining, many of us forget to make the most of it. However, once you wake up to the power you have to define your time as you wish, you can start to consciously take back control of the direction of your life. Large numbers of people go through life on autopilot and never really discover their wasteful attitude until it's too late.

People-pleasers have made a lifelong habit of putting other people first, being overly generous with their time and energy. The more of a people-pleaser you are, the more you're likely to unwittingly sacrifice your own time and energy to accommodate other people's needs.

When this happens, 'me time' becomes an occasional treat. Something that by definition feels like a rare pleasure, a luxurious extra rather than a necessary part of your everyday existence. But we're cheating ourselves by constraining our individual needs. In fact, to feel balanced, we all need some 'me time' every day. Quiet time to think, breathe and just be. We don't need to excuse this need, or dress it up. It's a fundamental necessity. There are 1,440 minutes in a day, so it doesn't seem too much to ask to find 30 for some 'me time'...

After blocking out time for yourself, the next step is to protect it. This time should be sacred. There will be distractions. Maybe a request for a favour, a last-minute meeting or an inconvenient reschedule. However, these people are asking you rather than instructing you. Pause before you answer.

Treat your own needs with the same respect you give to other people's. Whether it's lunch alone, half an hour spent reading or a walk listening to music, it's the space you need to recharge. Everyone around you will benefit from it, as you'll be more positive and energised as a result. It's win-win.

Each day is a moment in your lifetime. With the average life span in the UK being 82 years, that translates to approximately 30,000 days. Not many days – especially when you consider that a 40 year old has only around 15,000 days remaining. A very compelling reason to value your time even more!

Rule #3: Be RELENTLESS

The difference between success and failure in life is a combination of perseverance and resilience. Cultivating an attitude of relentlessness ensures that your motivational momentum keeps spurring you on. Working on your authenticity and being ruthless about the way you spend your time will feed into this. Psychologists are now saying that the number one factor for a successful life is grit. This can be defined as a combination of determination and resolve.

Having a never-say-die attitude can potentially get you further and faster towards the life that you desire, if you decide 'enough is enough' and start pursuing your dreams with relentless drive and determination.

There are countless successful people who refused to give up in the face of obstacles that would have undermined the determination of most people. Here are a few of the best known and most inspiring examples:

- Elon Musk was bullied as a child in South Africa, and would later drop out of his Stanford PhD to set up his first company Zip2, before going on to be enormously successful at PayPal, SpaceX and Tesla.
- Former door-to-door fax machine sales rep Sarah Blakely, against the advice of all her doubters, put in $5,000 of

her own savings and launched a range of hosiery called Spanx. After disrupting the hosiery industry, she has gone on to become a billionaire.

- Ludwig van Beethoven was dismissed by his music teacher as 'hopeless as a composer'.
- The Beatles were rejected by Decca Records, with the head of A&R, Dick Rowe, telling Brian Epstein that guitar groups were 'on the way out'.
- Steven King's manuscript for *Carrie* was initially rejected for being non-commercial. It was rejected 30 times.
- Steven Spielberg was rejected three times from the same film school before going on to study elsewhere, then dropping out of his course.
- Fred Astaire received the damning verdict: "Can't act. Can't sing. Slightly bald. Can dance a little," after an audition at MGM. He went on to star in 31 musical films and become one of the biggest names of the age.
- Elvis Presley was told by the manager of the Grand Ole Opry, Jimmy Denny, "You ain't goin' nowhere, son. You ought to go back to drivin' a truck."
- J K Rowling was rejected by 12 publishers before the first Harry Potter novel got picked up.
- Oprah Winfrey was fired from her job as a TV news reporter early in her career, for being 'unfit for TV'.
- Michael Jordan was dropped from his high school basketball team for 'lack of skill'.

For most people, rejection is seen as something to be avoided at all costs. Rejection equals pain and to embrace it could be viewed as a sign of madness. The feelings associated with rejection will at some level have been developed in our childhood years. It is confused with a lack of love, which we essentially will always move away from.

Rather than look at rejection as the end of the road, it can be something to be embraced and celebrated. Why not give rejection a great big mental hug!? If you thought that on the other side of it was success, would you look at it differently? Would you become more relentless? Continually fearing rejection can ultimately keep you stuck. It might manifest as a fear of not being good enough, of not being loved, or of being exposed as a fraud or an imposter. All of these anxieties are far more damaging than the rejection itself.

What you will find is that when your message is greater than your fear, you overcome any feelings of rejection with greater ease. The famous examples above discovered their 'message' and were therefore not put off by the possibility of rejection. They were, in essence, on a mission. They were relentless.

Rule #4: Avoid Regret

What's the one word you'd like to avoid saying on the last day of your life? Probably 'regret'.

When somebody is struggling with a difficult situation – they're in a toxic relationship but can't seem to break away, or they're stuck in a career that fills them with dread every morning – I encourage them to think forward.

I ask them to imagine themselves on their deathbed, looking back over their life. What is it they feel sad about? What do they wish they had done differently? What do they wish they had done more of, and less of? For many people, this is a profound exercise, and can be incredibly helpful in gauging how true to their values and deep desires their life is in a given moment.

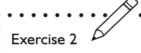

Exercise 2

Try it yourself. Write down the feelings that arise. How does your present situation look to you with this knowledge in mind? What do you need to change?

Bronnie Ware, a US-based palliative care nurse, wrote a book based on her experience of the top five regrets of the dying.

Here is what they were:

1. **'I wish I'd had the courage to live a life true to myself, not the life others expected of me.'**
   The most common regret, this reflected the regret dying people felt at not chasing their dreams and instead living the life mapped out for them.
2. **'I wish I hadn't worked so hard.'**
   Ware said that every male patient had this regret. They had worked at the expense of quality time with their families, missing children growing up and not spending the time they needed with their partner.
3. **'I wish I'd had the courage to express my feelings.'**
   In an effort to keep the peace, Ware says that many of her patients had repressed their deepest-held feelings. She believes that some developed illnesses as a consequence of the resentment caused by the pent-up emotion. Personally, I also believe that many men out there withhold their feelings and never seek help, as they try to avoid feeling embarrassment, shame and what they see as emasculation. In reality, vulnerability should be seen as a sign of strength.
4. **'I wish I had stayed in touch with my friends.'**
   Many dying patients reached a new awareness of the importance of friendship in their final days. Many said they had let life get in the way of maintaining bonds with people who were important to them.
5. **'I wish I had let myself be happier.'**
   Many of the dying said that, looking back over their lives, they could see that fear of change, pleasing others and the patterns they formed in life had prevented them from being happy.

Ware says, "When you're on your deathbed, what others think of you is a long way from your mind. How wonderful to be able to let go and smile again, long before you are dying. Life is a choice. It is your life. Choose consciously, choose wisely, and choose honestly. Choose happiness."

Grace Bluerock, who worked in hospice care for over six years, noted that people regretted:

- **'Not being more loving to the people who mattered.'**
  Suddenly, with regret, you realise that a lot of these people are gone and you never got a chance to let them know how much you loved them.
- **'Why did I worry so much?'**
  People regret that they spent so much time focusing on what they thought was wrong with life, worrying all the time instead of actually living life with zest and appreciation. As a consequence, they feel they missed the truth about what life was all about.

Just something for you to think about: what percentage of your worry has actually ever come true? Research indicates that it's about 10%. And according to Professor Gary Marcus of New York University, even worrying for five minutes can vastly dampen your spirits.

RULE #5: Learn to Relinquish

To relinquish is to surrender or let go of what you are holding on to. Imagine holding a small glass of water in your hand with your arm outstretched. Is it heavy? Of course not. It's just a glass of water! What would happen, though, if you were left standing there for three hours? Would the weight of the glass of water increase? No. But would your arm feel heavy? Yes – very possibly you would have put the glass down long before the three hours were up.

When you hold on to an emotion from the past, it has a similar effect on your mind. That is why we say we feel 'weighed down'. The past seems to be a burden on us. This in turn puts us in a low mood. If you look at someone who is feeling down or suffering from depression, how do they tend to stand or walk? Do they stand up straight or slightly bent over?

> A lady lost her grandson in a car accident in early 2004. At the time, all her friends rallied around her to comfort and console her. All these years later, if you were to have a conversation with this lady, I'm told within minutes of you starting talking to her, she will start mentioning her grandson. And this will continue through the conversation. It has become seemingly impossible for friends and family to talk to her as she is now living in some kind of carousel of torture. Imagine her standing at the centre. Although you may be talking to her, she can only see the images of her grandson, represented by the horses flashing by on the outer part of the carousel. No matter what you say, she is still distracted by the past and the question 'What if…?'

Letting go is something that people find difficult. People get into heated arguments and then do not seem to be able to let go after the argument finishes. This could lead to a grudge forming. The quicker you can let go of anything, the quicker you can move forward in life.

 TIP: Write the five individual rules on a post-it note and keep it in your purse or wallet.

Case study

Ashley

I had a client back in 2014 who was brought in to see me by his wife of 15 years. The client was obsessed with losing his wife and was suffering control issues. This was resulting in them experiencing very difficult times in their relationship, and nearing possible break-up. After a couple of sessions, I discovered that his parents had split up when he was 11 years old, but prior to that he had seen them warring for two years. This had created considerable uncertainty and doubt in his mind, which he replayed unconsciously during his own marriage – hence the controlling behaviour towards his wife. Discovering this to be the root cause was like an epiphany to him. Immediately, he decided to let go of that old story he was telling himself and relinquish the need to control his wife. He embraced the 'Let It Go' and 'Where Focus Goes, Energy Flows' Power Statements, understanding that if he focused on trust and the value of his relationship, things would work out.

Similarly, the ability to let go of the future can lead to a lowering of anxiety and worry. After all, worry is primarily based in the future. We have this innate ability to focus continually on future events and how we picture them happening. Have you ever been lying there at night playing an imaginary conversation in your head with someone? As you continue this conversation in your head, you start to work yourself up into a state! We play these conversations or scenarios in our mind and unknowingly change our state from calm to anxiety within seconds.

The act of letting go and renouncing the need to control the future can provide a source of relief. 'Let It Go' applies to the past and the future. What happens if you relinquish the need to focus on the past or future? You end up firmly focused on the present and what's around you.

17

What Next?

'For me, becoming isn't about arriving somewhere or achieving a certain aim. I see it instead as forward motion, a means of evolving, a way to reach continuously toward a better self. The journey doesn't end.'"
~ Michelle Obama

My main aim in writing this book was to try to provide you with insight, and hope that you will be able to understand how and why you think the way you do. Even the realisation and awareness that understanding this is important is, for many people, enough to bring about a change in the way they think.

It would be remiss of me not to assist you in answering that burning question, 'What do I do next?' I always believe that simply possessing the tools and know-how is not enough. You have to practise and keep implementing them to unlock their full power. I truly believe in their effectivity in enabling mindset and emotional change.

Certain methods and tools contained in this book will apply to your life right now. You may feel the benefits from the other tools at another point in the future. It all depends at what stage you are in your life, and what challenges you have to overcome. For example, when I've polled previous clients, many people have reported a particular Power Statement resonating with them. I'm wondering which one has resonated with you?

Exercise

Answer the following questions and make a decision to let go of something that you now feel you have to, and can, leave behind. It could be a bad habit that is costing you money; a behaviour like people-pleasing which is making you resentful; or trying to avoid coming out of your comfort zone, which is stifling your business. Whatever it is, everyone has something to let go of. They often don't even realise this, as they are consumed with the rigmarole of everyday life.

1. What is it critical for you to let go of? (e.g. procrastinating, people-pleasing, blaming others)

2. How is it impacting on your life? (e.g. feel angry, feel helpless, headaches)

3. What has it cost you so far? (e.g. relationships, business growth, fitness, health, happiness, money)

4. What will happen if you don't resolve this habit, thinking or behaviour?

5. What will be the impact on your life if you do let go?

TIP: It is even more effective if you have an accountability partner when you are doing this challenge. If your friend doesn't have a copy of this book, you can always surprise them and gift them a copy.

I'm now going to challenge you to the 100-Day Challenge. This is designed for you to efficiently utilise the contents of this book, helping both yourself and others at the same time. The world needs more love, joy and peace. The process of letting go can help that change become reality.

Stage 1: Days 1–30

Read the entire contents of this book again. (Divide the number of pages by 30, and read that approximate number per day.)

After each chapter, write brief notes about the most important points in a small notebook.

Stage 2: Days 31–60

In this 30-day period, focus on a minimum of three aspects from the book, e.g. the Power Statements, the Attitude of Gratitude, the Letter, and teach them to someone. This may be a family member, friend or colleague, but pick someone who you think may be receptive to learning from you. Whenever you teach something, you learn it yourself again, reinforcing the knowledge within you.

Stage 3: Days 61–70

Focus again on a chapter which you feel connected to at that moment. Focus on practising the content of this chapter, e.g. stopping blaming, complaining, judging.

Stage 4: Days 71–100

For this period, go through the notes in your notebook with either the person from Stage 2, or someone entirely new.

Values

Acceptance
Accountability
Accuracy
Achievement
Acknowledgement
Activeness
Adaptability
Advancement
Adventure
Affection
Alertness
Altruism
Ambition
Appreciation
Approachability
Approval
Articulacy
Assertiveness
Assurance
Attentiveness
Attractiveness
Availability
Awareness

Balance
Being the best
Belonging
Bravery

Calmness
Capability

Care
Carefulness
Caution
Certainty
Challenge
Change
Charm
Chastity
Cheerfulness
Clarity
Cleanliness
Clear-mindedness
Cleverness
Closeness
Comfort
Commitment
Community
Compassion
Competence
Competition
Composure
Concentration
Confidence
Conformity
Connection
Consistency
Contentment
Continuity
Control
Coolness
Cooperation

Correctness
Courage
Courtesy
Creativity
Credibility
Cunning
Curiosity

Decisiveness
Deference
Depth
Desire
Determination
Devotion
Dignity
Diligence
Discipline
Discovery
Discretion
Diversity
Dominance
Dreaming
Drive
Duty
Dynamism

Ease
Economy
Education
Effectiveness
Elegance

Empathy

Encouragement

Endurance

Energy

Enjoyment

Entertainment

Enthusiasm

Environmentalism

Ethics

Excellence

Experience

Expertise

Expressiveness

Fairness

Faith

Fame

Family

Fashion

Fearlessness

Fidelity

Financial freedom

Firmness

Fitness

Flexibility

Flow

Focus

Frankness

Freedom

Friendliness

Friendship

Fun

Gallantry

Generosity

Giving

Grace

Gratitude

Gregariousness

Growth

Guidance

Happiness

Hard-working

Harmony

Health

Heart

Helpfulness

Heroism

Honesty

Honour

Hopefulness

Hospitality

Humility

Humour

Hygiene

Imagination

Independence

Individuality

Influence

Insightfulness

Inspiration

Integrity

Intelligence

Intensity

Intimacy

Introspection

Intuitiveness

Inventiveness

Involvement

Joy

Justice

Kindness

Knowledge

Leadership

Learning

Lightness

Liveliness

Logic

Longevity

Love

Loyalty

Making a difference

Marriage

Mastery

Maturity

Meaning

Meekness

Mellowness

Mindfulness

Modesty

Motivation

Mysteriousness

Nature

Neatness

Nerve

Obedience

Objectivity

Open-mindedness

Openness

Optimism

Order

Organisation

Originality

Outdoors

Partnership
Passion
Patience
Patriotism
Peace
Perceptiveness
Perfection
Perseverance
Persuasiveness
Pleasure
Poise
Popularity
Power
Practicality
Pragmatism
Precision
Preparedness
Presence
Pride
Privacy
Proactivity
Professionalism
Prosperity
Punctuality
Purity

Rationality
Realism
Reason
Reasonableness
Refinement
Reflection
Relaxation
Reliability
Reputation
Resilience
Resourcefulness

Respect
Responsibility

Sacrifice
Satisfaction
Science
Security
Self-control
Selflessness
Self-reliance
Self-respect
Sensitivity
Sensuality
Serenity
Service
Sexuality
Sharing
Shrewdness
Silence
Silliness
Simplicity
Sincerity
Skilfulness
Solidarity
Solitude
Sophistication
Speed
Spirituality
Spontaneity
Stability
Status
Stillness
Strength
Structure
Success
Support
Sympathy

Teaching
Teamwork
Thankfulness
Thoroughness
Thoughtfulness
Tidiness
Traditionalism
Trust
Trustworthiness
Truth

Understanding
Unflappability
Unity
Usefulness

Valour
Variety
Virtue
Vision

Warmth
Winning
Wisdom
Wittiness
Worthiness

Youthfulness

Zeal

Please feel free to add others of your own!

For further resources, please go to the website

www.davidrahman.life

where you can access more content to enhance
your understanding of mindset, human behaviour
and the process of letting go.
I also post regularly on Instagram (david_rahman)
and Facebook (Mind Coach).